I0822581

HIMALAYAN TRAVELS
SIKKIM, KULU AND LAHOUL
1950 - 51

John Meredith Williams

Edited by Tobias Lescht and Cecily Hennessy

For Jean Constance Williams
on her ninetieth birthday
29th June 2018

'The whole afternoon's expedition was more in the nature of
exercise than climbing as there was nothing much to be seen which
had not been seen before and nothing much to do
but climb up or down – and in that lay the joy,
the joy of just existing
in a perpendicular world.'

John Meredith Williams

Published by Cecily Hennessy Publications

First edition, 2018.

ISBN 978-0-9576628-2-7

Frontispiece: John Meredith Williams, 1951
Endpiece: And those who did the work, 1950

CONTENTS

Preface vii

Sikkim, October 1950 9

Illustrations 57

Kulu and Lahoul, May - June 1951 79

Illustrations 127

Maps 148

List of Illustrations and Maps 151

4, BANKSHALL STREET,
CALCUTTA.

31/10/51.

Note to parents, Gwynne and Cicely Williams 31/10/51

This is very much overdue I am afraid. There was great delay in finishing the typing & I have been sitting on it for the last few weeks. However I hope you're enjoying having a glance at it. The photographs are not very good but do at least give some idea of what the country looks like --and that is magnificent! In case you are getting worried I have shaved that gruesome looking beard!

Let's hope this arrives in time for Christmas.

Johnny

PREFACE

John Meredith Williams was born on 20th October 1926. After being educated at Sherborne School, Dorset and Trinity Hall, Cambridge, he served in the Royal Signals and then worked for Shaw Wallace and Company Ltd., based in Calcutta.

As a young man, in 1950 and 1951, he made two excursions into the Himalayas, the first with his friend Charles Stanley. He recorded his travels in journals, which on returning to Calcutta, he typed and illustrated with photographs and sent to his parents, Gwynne and Cicely Williams, who were then living in Kimpton, Hertfordshire.

We have transcribed the journals, which reflect the age in which they were written, and no attempt has been made to adapt them for a contemporary audience.

Johnny always loved the mountains but as he said himself, 'I have come to the conclusion that I will never make anything of a Himalyan climber as I am always far too keen on seeing round the corner—and there is always a corner round which has not been inspected before.'

Tobias Lescht
Cecily Hennessy
New York, May 2018

SIKKIM

OCTOBER 1950

My journeys commenced on the 28th September 1950 when I left Rajnandgaon for Bombay on a business visit, but it did not begin to count until I landed at Dum Dum at about twelve o'clock on the morning of Saturday the 30th. Fortunately the journey had been a smooth one after we had crossed the Western Ghats and I was well both in body and soul. The trip in to Calcutta from the aerodrome was even more depressing than usual as we arrived in a sharp shower of rain whereas we had flown in perfect weather for most of the way over India.

The boredom of the bus journey was slightly relieved by chaffing the hostess with the inefficiency of her service and so it was not all that long before we were turned out at the Great Eastern. By a miracle of organisation there was an office car waiting for me and though it took a bit of time for me to recognise it as such, I was soon piled in and on my way out to Bondel Road. There they had given me up more or less as lost and so no time – not even drinking time – was wasted before sitting down to tiffin. The programme for the evening was extensive as there were numerous things to be bought, as well as a lot of my kit to be collected from Alipore. The idea was that I was first to set out with CBS [Charles Stanley] to buy what remained of the stores and then to come back and start again with DMG [Don Gordon]. One trouble was that there was no very clear idea as to what stores were needed. However we went round to the Empire Stores and got some things which it occurred to us were deficient. After that a search was made for some socks for CBS but without much success and he had to be content with some pretty grim efforts. Wool socks seem to be off the market in Calcutta and American cotton mixture socks were the best that could be found.

When that was finished we went out to Alipore to collect my clothes but found that there was no one in who had a vital key so we had to retire discomfited. Back to Bondel Road and off with DMG on the camera search; his original ideas had fallen through as the camera which was wanted had disappeared from the market and we were forced to consider the matter afresh. The only things which were available and of the right nature were a Rolleiflex and an Agfa. I decided to take the Agfa as being nearer the right size and shape for carrying round mountains, although against it was the fact that everyone advised against a 35 mm camera for my casual sort of use. This camera was bought at a 20% discount and together with the necessary accessories came to a fraction under Rs700. At this time I was still feeling the effects of Rajnandgaon Richness.

The next item on the programme was another visit to Alipore to try again to get the gear, which this time was available. By now it was getting on for night and a party had been scheduled to begin some time ago. My evening dress was in a shocking state having been in a box for the previous six months, but the idea was not to arrive at the Slap[1] until a late hour when no one should be in a fit state to notice such things. The time from eight till three, when I dropped into bed dead to the world had better be forgotten about. It was the height of the Rugger Week in Calcutta and the party reflected the spirit of the time. I had to pause to think whether I had come from, or to the

1 Saturday Club.

jungle. The others carried on till five or so and were in an appropriately bad state the next morning.

As the gods would have it I was feeling not so bad and was able to face the enormous amount of organisation which remained to be done without too much of a head. CBS did not turn up on the scene till nearly eleven and by the time he had finished breakfast it was time to go off to the Slap for a further round of refreshment. This was duly done and the same rowdy party was found to be in progress. Numerous rude comments were flying around on the state of my hair, which was admittedly a disgusting length. In due course we had absorbed enough to be refreshed and we left for tiffin at the US Club.[2] The others waded in to the curry but I was convinced that that would send me straight to sleep so I had some normal civilised food though it seemed strange stuff after the months of stewed goat and ladies' fingers at Rajnandgaon.

The afternoon was spent happily, if somewhat wearily, in packing the goods into their final containers and wondering if we had enough of anything. In the evening there was some more drinking to be done with CCL as I was to give him the report on my doings in Bombay. There was very much more drinking than business done that night.

It was an exceedingly tired JMW [John Meredith Williams], who flopped into bed after dinner that night with the thought uppermost in his mind that he was to get up at 5.15 the next morning. Sleep was very Sound.

Monday October 2nd. The trip really began in earnest this day when we left Calcutta. Of course the bearer failed to wake up at the right time but a combination of an alarm clock and the fact that I was awake anyway enabled us to get off to schedule.

Appropriately enough we left for the airport in the SW & Co Wines and Spirits van which we had scrounged the night before. It was a tight fit for three in the front and almost as tight a fit in the back, Calcutta was looking its usual self to say good-bye and that usual is a combination of filth and aroma unimaginable in Rajnandgaon. The final send-off was a dead and high buffalo lying by the side of the road which was not a good portent for the air journey. We arrived at Dum Dum a good while before the time of departure and entered into a long argument with the Airways people. It appeared that they were not prepared to take our excess baggage, which was 120 lbs strong, as the arrangements we had made for forward booking had not penetrated to the right quarters. Fortunately for tempers and for the success of the trip someone cancelled at the last moment and we were able to pile it all on. We had five items altogether: –

2 Allsopp's Lager boxes full of food.

1 Gunny sack full of tents and such like.

1 Bedding Roll.

1 Ruc-sac.

and they looked enough to equip a company for a month's campaign.

The plane was a Dakota and more or less on time we took off for Bagdogra. The trip took about an hour and a half and was most exceeding dull. The monsoon had not yet completely cleared away and there was a deal of cloud about some of which we ran into about half way along. The Fasten Belts' lighted up and we were flung around a bit although CBS managed to sleep through it all. The food was of a very low order – and served by a steward – but neither of us worried much about such things at this end of the trip.

---

2 United Services Club, now the Bengal Club.

In due course we made an awful landing at Bagdogra. The air strip is a very kutcha[3] affair of matting and it is remarkable that it stands up to all the battering it gets from 20-25 planes a day, but even so the way we felt the bumps meant that the pilot was a bit kutcha too.

The air-port facilities are non-existent and everyone just hung around to see what happened. We were approached by a Ceylon tea planter and his wife on the subject of taking a car, but at the time our economical mind ran on buses. After a long time it became evident that the airline had an arrangement for transport to Darjeeling at a mere Rs12 a head. Once we knew about this we all piled in to a Ford station wagon and cancelled a previous tentative bandobast[4] at double the price. As luck would have it there was just enough room for the two of us, the tea planter and his hard, but hard, wife, and a padre who read his Bible all the way up and cursed all and sundry on the slightest delay. From the air-port there is a little way to go along the Siliguré road and then one turns off to the left and within five miles is climbing up through the steaming jungle into the foot hills. The road is quite good and our Ford took most of it at speed. The road twists and turns a great deal but does not have the spectacular quality of some of the lesser or for that matter of the main roads in the Alps. On the lower stretches there is no damage to speak of and we quickly mounted to the regions of cloud and cool. The DHR[5] follows the road for most of the way and we saw a number of the silly little engines fussing up and down. The railway is now run as a shuttle service as far as the main breach, although they are cleaning the line up beyond the breach as though they intended to open some time.

Before long a great accumulation of trucks and cars and people came in sight and our car was surrounded by milling coolies. This was the great break in the road where 200 yds of it is sliding and has slid down to the valley below. They have not yet taken any steps to put it right confining their attention to getting the stuff across with the greatest ease, for which purpose they have put up a rope-way along which the Darjeeling bound bags of rice may slide. Before we could say a word our kit was away and being taken over to the far side. At this stage, we did not know whether our arrangements were for transport through to Darjeeling or not and the porters seemed to have little idea either. They pressed on regardless though and quite a little way beyond the far side of the slip we came to a bazaar, where there were parked a large number of cars two of which appeared to be the other half of the bandobast. Then followed a long argument with the coolies about their pay. They claimed Rs1 for their trouble and we estimated 8as[6] as their due; so we gave them 9as for luck. They have been completely spoilt by the slips and have an exaggerated idea of the value of their service. Immediately after the slip a coolie could make Rs100 a day in this game. The top bit of the road is much the shorter but is damaged in places on the way up to Ghoom. The cloud was still all around us and we had no good view of anything; indeed we had not seen much all the way up from the plains. From Ghoom onwards the road goes downhill to Darjeeling and on this side of the ridge the air was clear and one could see the wooded foothills of Sikkim, that part of Sikkim which CBS had previously been to.

On our arrival in Darjeeling, we sought the advice of the priest as to the chances of getting action out of the DCs office on this day as it was some sort of a holiday. He recommended a visit

---

3 Crude.

4 Arrangement.

5 Darjeeling Himalayan Railway.

6 16as = Rs1.

to one Mr Kidd who was alleged to know all about these things. We had directions to his house and after a great deal of effort on the steep hills we reached it, to be let in by his wife to a house belonging to a past age and a different continent. Kidd himself was ill, recovering from the effects of a chill, and we were shown through to his stuffy bedroom where he was lying back well wrapped up in all sorts of long forgotten garments. He was a pleasant enough old man but full of depression. He thought that there was nothing to be done that day; that we would need our passports which were in Calcutta; that one could not get a pass to Gangtok to go and arrange about a trek in Sikkim, but that all the details had to be fixed first; that they were very sticky about visits to the neighbourhood of the Tibetan border; and a whole host of other things which put together would mean that our trip was about done for. Fortunately we only believed a small part of what he said even at the time, and he was able to clarify our ideas on where to go. The original scheme had been to go to Mome Samdong and make an attempt to cross the Karpo La which I at that time believed – wrongly – not to have been crossed before. This plan would mean that we were near the Tibet border for a long time and not on any recognised route. It was thought, therefore, that this would not have the approval of the powers that be. The plan that seemed the more likely from that point of view and also to provide some fun was to cross the Donkya La and spend a long time on the high level traverse before dropping down to Thangu. Even so it was likely that there would be some time to spare which could be filled in by short trips with Thangu as the base. This was not a very exciting programme but at the best of times it was for the officials mainly and we did not intend to stick to it rigidly if we found something more original to do. Whatever the plans might be on arrival in Sikkim however, the first thing to be done was to get to Gangtok.

Put off by the gloomy predictions of Mr Kidd we gave up all hope of getting on that day and retreated to a cafe for some eats. From there we betook ourselves to the Guest House Johannes where CBS had previously stayed. It was rather tawdry but we were neither of us feeling strong enough for the Everest. After installing ourselves we went down to the bazaar to see if we could find out anything about the transport situation. We did find that there was a jeep service to Kalimpong twice daily, the road being in fair condition. We also found that no one had any idea about how to get to Gangtok. There appeared to be a block at the 19th milestone from Gangtok, beyond which, though it was alleged the road was open, no one had any clear idea of what was happening. The answer could only be to go and see. It was raining periodically and the town was looking dreary, though not much landslide damage was to be seen. We went round to the bazaar and bought one or two useful items like Dubbin,[7] and found that it was a much more cheerful place than the New Market [Calcutta]. Indeed I was much impressed by the town for its cheerful aspect being – after months in the jungle at Nandgaon – knocked more or less senseless by the Nepali girls.

We had an early meal back at the Boarding House and were very glad of the fire which was laid on. The meal was enormous and we were only just able to compete with it. Then it was straight to bed and the best night's sleep for a long time, quite catching up on the losses of the previous nights.

Tuesday October 3rd. We were awake at an early hour – or what was an early one for us at this stage, and went out for a walk. We went straight up the road, being offered many ponies on the way and round the north end of the ridge. It was a glorious morning, fresh and with a few clouds floating inconsequently around. We caught a glimpse of Kanchenjunga, though not all of it at one

7 Wax used to waterproof.

time and marvelled, as does everyone, at how far it is above the wooded hills opposite. We were somewhat consoled by the thought that we would – if we got to Sikkim which seemed then at best problematical – just about split the difference in the heights. On the way back we got involved in the grounds of Government House, nearly taking a jungle track down the khud-side[8] to the Rangit but thought better of it at this early stage of the trip.

Back to another large meal and then in search of the DC's office – which rejoiced in the name of Kutchery. This was at last traced miles down a broad high road to the north of the bazaar and in no time we were installed in the office of the DI Fund. There we discovered that the vital man had had the pass all the time and that we could have got hold of it the day before by going down to his house. This was a bit peeving but we were so pleased and relieved to have the thing anyway that we did not worry much about the lost time. As it was by now nearly eleven it was high time to get a move on the way to Kalimpong. At this stage we thought it possible that we night get to Gangtok that night. The official jeep had gone a long time ago and so we went into the bazaar and asked for transport. The main candidates were an Austin A40 and an extremely battered jeep, the former to Kalimpong and the latter to the block at the nineteenth mile. After the usual haggling which ended by tossing the man for the last Rs5 we chose the jeep and were heartily glad we had done so. It was to cost us Rs70 up to the slip and at that time we thought it excessive but having seen the road we thought it cheap. The bandobast being made we toured the town to get hold of some petrol and all our goods which were scattered between the lodging house and the garage where we first arrived. This took only a short time but showed us the state of repair of the jeep which was shaky; one had to start her by rolling down the hill, there was no spare wheel, and she rattled even more than GWL 850.

The route started off up the road to Ghoom there turning left and going down the north side of the ridge. The road is narrow and while patched in some places is negotiable for a jeep. The view to the north across the Rangit was first class; the steep wooded slopes amazing us by their length and abruptness. The villages tend to be on the ridges of the spurs in lovely airy situations; but how they fix their water supply is more than I can say. On our side of the valley there was a series of tea estates including the famous Lokchu, which was also the name of the only bazaar on the road. I had never seen tea before at this range and was amazed at how flat topped the bushes were. Nor did I realise that the bushes grew in grass. I suppose that the hoeing away is either for young tea only or a complete line of bull. The tea garden staff in this part of the world must keep fit enough as these gardens were just about vertical in places.

Up at the top end of the road it was cool and fresh but by the time we were coming down the final spur above the Tista through the forest it was hot and wet again, Tista Bridge being only just about the thousand mark. The village of Tista Bazaar was a wreck with many of the houses leaning drunkenly about as though they were about to drop into the river at any moment. This was all damage caused by the flood. The road was nearly blocked at this point by a subsidence but the bridge itself was in order. This is not surprising as it is firmly based on rock at each side and is just one massive concrete span. It really is a very impressive piece of work, and the river will have to get a lot of work on if it wants to wash that into the sea. We crossed over without stopping and set off on the climb to Kalimpong. It was only at this stage that we realised that the first bit of the Gangtok road was down and that we had to go on over the hill from Kalimpong along a private

8 Gully/ravine-side.

road. My ideas on the geography of this part were hazy in the extreme but seeing it in the flesh made life a lot easier, giving a form to the tumbling contours. The maps with their steep slopes and a mass of names are difficult to read without an excess of concentration. The jeep managed to get up the hill without stopping to cool off though it got very hot in the process and I was watching the thermometer anxiously most of the way.

Kalimpong is a lovely town, which though a little lower than Darjeeling is smaller and of a more English appearance. We went straight to the parking lot at the back of the main street and de-camped into the nearest Chinese restaurant. The food was not sparkling but we were hungry and it was soon wolfed down. By now it was nearly half past two and time was pressing so after only half an hour we moved on. From here the road goes along the east side of the valley, high above the river below. This valley is a wide open one compared to that of the Rangit. It was not a good road but all the streams which crossed the road ran on concrete aprons which is the latest scream in road design in this part of the world. Being the main trade route we passed strings of ponies on their way to Tibet. The trade is said to be wool one way and salt and nails the other. In a few miles we turned left off the main road and climbed up to the ridge passing a forest bungalow. From the ridge the road coasts northward down to the Tista through the Government Chinchona plantation. Half way down we came to the Manager's bungalow where he was waiting to see that we did not use his extra special private road but only that which was merely private. This again required a lot of round about Hindi to find out from our driver, especially as he had hoped to worm his way through and go down the other shorter route. Not much later we were down in the valley and back on the proper road which though not much better was a little wider. Indeed it started off by taking a short cut across the river bed which required four wheel drive to negotiate.

Rangpo is the border station and there we had to sign the book and hand in part of our passes on the Indian side and on the other we had merely to sign the Sikkim police report which follows one to all the organised parts of the state. These formalities were soon done and we began the last lap straight up the valley to the break at the 19th mile. Just before that, there was a dak[9] bungalow which was a temptation, but we decided to press on at least to the bungalow at Martam which is at the 13th mile.

It was five when we arrived at the slip and there was no sign of life at all; our hopes of getting to Gangtok that night were finally shattered. As we were letting this sink in three of four weedy looking fellows slouched up and they were persuaded to take the kit on. We were under the impression that the arrangement was for all the way to the bungalow, but they thought to Singtam only. This is the village where the Chu meets the Tista and where the road turns right to climb up to Gangtok. The bungalow is another six miles on; a fact which we lightly dismissed believing that Singtam would be alive with transport. It was only a quarter of an hour's walk into the village which is only a muddy 'T' junction lined with dirty shops. It was dusk by now and we were warm and sticky and the whole place had a most depressing air about it.

When the coolies came up it was evident that they thought that they had done enough and so the goods were dumped by the side of the road and further labour was canvassed. They were an idle and insolent crowd and asked fantastic prices for the trip up to the bungalow, bidding began at Rs10 per man. We showed no signs of biting at that rate and a bullock cart was suggested. This started at Rs30 but worked its way down to Rs20 at which price we bought as we were heartily fed

---

9 Post.

up with the inhabitants of Etam and were willing to be stung if only we could leave them behind. Having seen the goods loaded on to the cart and having agreed to pay the coolies an exorbitant sum Rs1 each for their ¼ hrs work, we set off up the road. Before we had gone more than a few hundred yards it was dark and we had to feel our way along. It was easy on the dirt sections as the track showed light against the jungle, but the tarmac was more tricky except where it was wet and reflected the sky. Before long all the road was wet as it started raining and went on and on all the way up. We were joined outside Singtam by a curious fellow who claimed that he was looking for work in Gangtok, but whose motives we strongly suspected. He was not apparently very bright either and we got no information of use out of him, though we were badly in need of gen about everything. On the road there is a short tunnel of most forbidding appearance and as black as a coal cellar. We were heartily glad to emerge from that one – as was our companion to judge by the efforts he made to keep up with us on the way through. On the way back it looked tame enough but in the dark it was a very different proposition.

At about half past six we really could not see the way at all and had to resort to the torch though we were keen on saving the battery as much as possible. I was walking on the outside and was shattered to see the precipices, which I had avoided falling over when steering on instinct. At seven we got to the bungalow and yelled loudly for the chowkidar.[10] He came up in fair time but proved to be one of those who apparently live on dry rice and water. At length he agreed to slaughter a chicken and curry it for us. At the same time he lit a fire and we were able to dry out a little. He also produced some tea which was horrible but at least warm. Our walking companion came in and made himself at home by the fire and had eventually to be ejected more or less forcibly. He was seen in the morning in the chowkidar's hut looking a bit lost but he did not worry us any further. I think he must have been merely a bit soft in the head and not really of evil intention.

The chicken when it arrived had been cut into exceeding small bits so that we could not see how little of the beast we had got, and so that we should have difficulty in sorting the flesh from the bone. These fellows must eat bone and all. However we were hungry and though we did not like the idea of the rogue getting away with it so easily we did not care very much. The sleeping bags, as luck would have it were on the top of the boxes and we were soon lined up for bed. It was an uncomfortable night as it could not make up its mind whether it was hot or cold and sleeping bags work on the all or nothing principle. On balance it was hot.

Wednesday October 4th. We woke very early in the morning and in due course the chowkidar brought some tea and boiled eggs which was to do for our breakfast. We had tried the night before to find out from him what the transport situation was like though with little success. We had discovered that there was another block a mile up the road where two State lorries were stuck. This block was alleged to be going to be cleared very early in the morning and the lorries were then going on to Gangtok. The block was only a temporary one and the dak bus had been going through regularly including that afternoon. It was of no use to us though as it went up to Gangtok at three or four in the afternoon. In fact we had just missed it the day before though in the circumstances there was nothing we could have done to arrive at the block any earlier than we did. The idea at this stage was for us to walk into Gangtok if all else failed and send the coolies back for the goods. This would put us back for a whole day, but at this early hour we were rather depressed and accepted such a suggestion resignedly. After breakfast we left our kit at the mercy of the chowkidar

10 Watchman.

and walked up the road. It went round by the river which was boiling merrily away only a little way below, and then climbing and turning came into the village where the lorries were parked. Here began the usual bargaining only in this case they were not merely idle but in fear of their master the State Engineer. However with the aid of some mild bullying they were persuaded to turn back and pick up the goods from the bungalow. This did not take long once the talking had been finished and we were thankfully away on the last lap of the journey. We were split between the two lorries and CBS being on the faster one was well away. In another half an hour we were at the road block. I should have said that the road was still 'band'[11] but it was declared to be safe. An enormous boulder had fallen across the road and had been blown up without much luck leaving most of itself in the middle of the road. The outer wheels ran round on some stones perched on the edge of the abyss while the near side scraped the rocks. We wanted to suggest that our kit was unloaded but thought that it might be a bit tactless.

After this episode the road is quite tame and in places of excellent quality. In a few miles it crosses to the other bank and begins the climb up to Gangtok. This stretch has a number of zig-zags in it and is mostly plain hard work for the transport. Near the top my lorry began to show signs of wear and ceased to pull. Although it was not immediately obvious the trouble was that there was no petrol. Luckily for our conscience it was not the lorry which we had caused to go back for our goods. But also luckily for my legs it was the lorry which was carrying some petrol; so we were away again after only a small delay. However before the trouble had been traced to the lack of petrol I had begun to walk and in taking a short cut had collected and removed a number of leeches from my boots. It was my first introduction to these exceedingly horrible beasts though not a lethal introduction. Further up the hill the lorry stalled again and the same remedy of removing the air filter was tried without success. This time I had begun to walk again being fed up with standing and doing nothing. I did not have far to go again before I was caught up by the lorry and once again transported in relative cool. Even at this time of day it was quite hot although there was a freshness in the air not found in the lower regions.

At about half past nine I rolled into Gangtok and unloaded outside the shop of Jetmull Bhojraj who is the agent whom SW & Co deal with in Gangtok. He is also the State Banker and altogether a man to be made use of. CBS had been there some time and had managed to decline an invitation to tea from the manager. Some of our coolies had already turned up and on being told that this was the 'Angtharkay ke bandobast' had shouldered the goods and gone off to the bungalow. Soon after I arrived the sirdar[12] came down and we got the whole thing teed up. What we were really in need of was some breakfast and a shave. This was soon laid on and we emerged fit for the fray and determined that we should not have another shave until we returned to Gangtok. We had a hefty programme of organising ahead of us, so we wasted little time and returned to the bazaar and were directed thence to the Secretariat. Gangtok is built on a hill which faces NE with a line of important buildings along the top. At the N end is the Secretariat, then the Palace, then the Dewan's[13] bungalow then the Dak Khana, and finally in the most glorious of situations the PO's bungalow. We started off at the Secretariat and went to see the state Engineer to apologise for the two sins committed in the previous 24 hours. Luckily he condoned them both without quibble

11 Closed.

12 Man in charge.

13 Official.

but he was not saying anything on the further programme referring us to the Dewan who was at the time out of town, but he was alleged to be coming back at two o'clock or so. Next, on the list was the Superintendent of Police cum Officer in Charge Rationing. Here we stopped a rocket for the quality of the flour last sent up by United but we thought it tactful to forget to take the proffered sample. What we wanted from him was a permit to buy the coolie food and some of our own food in the bazaar and we had no difficulty in getting that. Our next stop was at the APO's office which is just below that of the PO, and right at the other end of Gangtok. We were learning the geography rapidly. He was delighted to see us but regretted that he could not see his way to extending the Sikkim pass until we had seen the Dewan and got his permission for the trek. On that we retired to the bungalow and had some lunch which we thought we well deserved.

At three o'clock we climbed back up to the Dewan's bungalow and were glad to see him working in his study. We were shown straight in and started on a long session about all sorts of things of which our own Trek was the least. He himself had just come back from a trip to Lachung in which he had gone over the Natu La to Yatung and from there over the Thangya La into Lachung. The whole trip was carried out at the most fantastic pace. He said that the normal road up the Tista was quite possible which was in contradiction to the gloomy stories we had heard up to date. He at least had no illusions as to what could and could not be done. We learnt a very great deal in our talk with this most charming man and ended up by being shown his photographs over some afternoon tea. I put my big hoof in it by asking his daughter the name of her teddy bear and being greeted by a flood of tears; apparently she thought that I was going to take it away from her. As an afterthought we collected a note from him saying in the best Civil Service jargon that we were allowed to do so. This was a magic document and excusing ourselves hurriedly we rushed down to the bazaar which was on the point of closing and grabbed our rations. The main item was nearly two maunds[14] of rice for the coolies.

It was nearly dusk by then and our next appointment was with the State Engineer at the Club at six. The Club as one might guess is at the top of the hill and is a very imposing building with little inside. In fact there was only a busy billiard table, a dreary collection of butterflies and assorted trophies of the hunt. Again as one might guess the man was late but when he did arrive he immediately wrote out our requirements in the way of passes on the back of a letter and sent it round to his head clerk who was to have it ready at his office at an early hour of the morning. Having done that there was only one thing left – to get our pass extended to the end of the month. This also was easy as it had only to be sent round to the APO by hand and it came back duly signed in half an hour. We found that the people of Gangtok were just dying for someone to talk to and if you could talk enough you were likely to get what you wanted. We spent most of the day talking.

The evening was given over to eating and organising the loads for the porters. When everything was put together there was an enormous amount of stuff and we were very doubtful if the chaps would take it all as their total load was close on 100 lbs including their own kit. The sirdar did not worry though so we merely filled our own sacks too full and hoped. The rest of the evening passed easily enough, although the rest of the bungalow was filled with hermits.

We slept again like logs and awoke early in the morning.

Thursday October 5th. Our aim had been to get away at half past seven and so we announced that we were going at seven. We got away – all of us – at half past seven so we said to

14 Unit of mass.

ourselves that this was a highly efficient expedition. We had a first stop very soon as we dropped off at the office of the State Engineer to pick up the passes. From Gangtok one should be able to see a white mountain – indeed the Dewan has had a tree especially cut to improve the view – but this morning we were only allowed a very small glimpse of such things. As it appears over a low wooded ridge it seems to be of another world and not really connected with the grisly task of getting down to Dikchu.

The bungalow passes were nearly ready and had been sent off to the State engineer for signature. We shelled out a number of shekels but got good value for them by the finish. The road to the Pedong La goes more or less level along the side of the hill and then climbs up to the Pass which is about 1,000 ft above the bazaar. We had not been going for a quarter of an hour before we overtook the coolies sitting by the side of the road, smoking; they do not believe in arriving early at the other end. We were going like bombs at this time of day and stopped only to take the picture of a water-powered prayer wheel which was busily engaged in turning out prayers to the gods. On our return it was having a day off so I presume that the gods are liable to get bored if they hear the same thing over and over again. The road is a broad metalled highway fit to take many cars though there cannot be one a day on it at the moment. The final few feet up to the Pedong La are quite steep and it was getting warm by now. The top of the pass itself is a prayer-flag bedecked defile[15] which gives straight away on to the next valley. The valley below Gangtok is a well inhabited place and almost the whole hillside below 5,000 ft is terraced with paddy fields. On the other side it is a bit more deserted and the road starts down through the jungle with a lovely view across the valley to some 14,000 ft wooded hills. At this stage we thought that they were marvellously high but in the next three weeks they became dwarfed. About half a mile down from the pass there is a small but well stocked bazaar and there the road changes from a marvellous one to merely a good one. It is possible to take a jeep as far as the pass and that is the form if one wants to make the double stage to Singhik in one day without being unduly energetic.

A little way below the village the road steepens and deteriorates where it crosses an old slip. A little further still there is a new slip which was our introduction to bad paths. It was only a small one but it took us a half hour to climb up and down again. Though a portion was very new the main part was of a year or two's standing and the deviation was of fair quality – good enough for mules at any rate. By this time I was getting hot and tired as the sack began to weigh heavily on the shoulders.

At this stage we parted and CBS pressed on with his light load while I made heavy weather of the path. There were a number of mule trains carrying alengee to Gangtok, some of it in the old flour bags from United. It took us a long time to find out what this alengee was though we soon came to recognise both the smell and the bushes on which it grows – it is actually cloves and is grown all over the Tista Valley below about 4,000 ft. The scenery on the way down to Dikchu is not very interesting as the forest grows steadily more and more exotic and the heat more and more sticky. I was soon reduced to a very sorry state and came to the conclusion that if there was one thing I really disliked it was walking in such hot and damp conditions.

Dikchu is a mere 1,700 ft above the sea and so one has a drop of about 4,500 ft on the first day after an easy climb of 1,000 ft. The distance is alleged to be thirteen miles and the mileposts were a source of great annoyance to me as they seemed to remind one of the painful slowness of

15 Narrow Pass.

progress. The road all the way to Lachen is lined with these posts but luckily quite a number of them have been washed away at one time or another; or met their fate in other ways and on quite large patches of track peace reigns. The bazaar at Dikchu is a depressing place nestling in the shade of some large trees at the junction of the Tista and the Dikchu. On enquiry the bungalow was said to be further along the road to Lachen and so I turned a weary step down to the Suspension Bridge. I think in that next quarter of a mile I asked the way three times – it was a highly populated area or I would not have seen so many people. The bungalow at last turned up perched on a ledge about a hundred feet above the raging Tista which makes a devil of a noise at this place and could be frightening when in spate I should think. CBS was well installed in an armchair drinking Andrews Liver Salts or some such in which I joined him. I was as near done as I like to be. I should really have taken a decent rest on the way down after which I would have gone very much better but such is my obstinacy in these things that I pressed on with very little rest and no food whatsoever.

The continual downward steps had damaged one big toe slightly but otherwise the new boots were a great success. The chowkidar was not quite so dumb as some and he laid on tea for us and later brought a few oranges from the tree in the bungalow garden. These latter were still green and we had some qualms about eating too many, though no ill effects were ever traced to them. CBS discovered that the bungalow had a stock of Saturday Evening Posts and he waded into these to the complete exclusion of the material world.

Dikchu is not a very pleasant place as one is completely shut in by the hills and the only consolation is the roaring river which at least provides good specimens of white water. The coolies turned up at about four without any signs of damage In fact, it is almost certain that the sahibs were the more damaged. The sirdar was a first class cook and he was at his best down in the lowlands where he could get all the things he wanted from the bazaar although we had to admit that on stores which had to be carried he was excellently economical. There was some panic about burglars and we slept with rather too many windows shut and what was hot any way became almost unpleasantly so.

Friday October 6th. Today's stage is to Singhik which is a net climb of 2,500 ft and twelve miles along the flat. That does not sound as though it should cause much difficulty but the truth is otherwise. It was again a day of hard work not all of which could be ascribed to the state of the road. Our morning programme at this stage was to have tea as soon as it was light, if not before, and get off as soon thereafter as could be, leaving the coolies to fend for themselves. In practise that meant tea at a quarter to five and a start somewhere well before seven. The last item on the duty list being to yell for the chowkidar and refuse to pay his demands. The greatest rogues live at the bottom. For instance the man at Martam tried to sting us Rs10 for his services; we paid Rs5. The man at Dikchu is not on a very good wicket as people do not want any wood there; so he makes up for it by trying to charge an exorbitant price for that which he does provide.

The first two miles along the river are easy enough with one waterfall to negotiate where the road has been washed into the river. This place is decorated by a fine specimen of a cane bridge which crosses over to some paddy fields on the other side of the river. Past the waterfall there follows a short good section and then we came to the first major effort – of which we had been warned. At the 15th milestone there is a big landslide – which we never saw – and the track to avoid it climbs up the hillside and passes through the beginnings of a village before dropping steeply back to the river near the liquor house at Ralak. Though we knew that there was a diversion we did not realise that we were to be asked to climb up the best part of a 1,000 ft of very steep hillside and then walk along an upsy downsy path for a mile or more before dropping through the thick forest, to the river. It was hot enough merely plodding along the valley bottom but as soon as we began to climb the sweat began to bout off in torrents. The day before I had tried to go without drinking on the march partly because it seemed likely that the water was bad and partly because in theory it is more comfortable, but my will power had collapsed by midday. This time I was having none of that nonsense and was going to drink whenever I felt that way, but even so my thirst was such that I still caught myself saying that I would have a drink at the next water hole but one and such, like signs of a raging thirst. Though it was hard work sweating up the hill in the full sunlight we went fairly well until we had dropped down to the river again at the drink house at Ralak. There we had a rest but no liquor. Thereafter it was just hard going, being one long grim slog. The path was not in a fit state for mules which meant that where there was a small slip one had to go up or down or both vertically rather than along a grade. On this section of the road there were many small slips and the grade was all the way against the engine. We were still on the map and could see where we were going until a bit beyond the suspension bridge. The map seemed to show that Mangan, through which we had to pass, was right down on the floor of the valley whereas the road left the other map at a height a 1,000 ft above the river. This was a bit disconcerting as we had visions of yet another 1,000 ft to slave up. As it was those final miles against the grade to Mangan were hard enough going, especially for CBS whose turn it was to carry the ruc-sac. Before we reached the bazaar and refreshment we were reduced to a stop and carry one sort of motion. Most of the way we were not in a good state to admire the view but what we did see was thrilling to eyes accustomed to the plains. The valley is steep at the bottom where there is just unadulterated jungle, while further up it opens out to make room for all the little paddy terraces as well as a bit to spare for bhuttas[16] and the occasional cow. Above that again come the wooded hills rising up into five figure heights.

Mangan is a line of shops which rudely turn their backs to the Talung Chu and rashly turn their fronts to the sun. They are faced by the Government offices headed by the dispensary. What is far more to the point is that one of the shops was producing tea which was a good approximation to Sergeant-major's. We drunk two cups each of this wonderful brew and were greatly refreshed. Meantime we talked to a fine old man who knew all about our arrival as he had himself come up from Dikchu that morning. The news of our arrival quite often preceded as by some unknown means although we walked at about the same speed as the average Sikkimese. This old fellow was very well equipped with a magnificent pair of boots, which might have graced any shooting party at home except that they were never done up. He claimed that he had come from Darjeeling and was on his way to Lachen where he had a house but apparently no work.

From Mangan to Singhik is only about three miles though they are all against the engine. The road is a really good one and climbs up at a steady pace with no diversion for landslides or for anything else. Going up one has the river on the left and an expanding view up the Talung Chu, a valley extremely deep cut and covered in jungle. I can well believe that higher up it is the most difficult of valleys to negotiate. If it is clear, one can see the peaks at the head of the valley from this path, but both in the afternoon and on the following morning there was heavy cloud about so we had not that refreshing sight.

The bungalow at Singhik is built just after the turn of the valley from N to NE and has an excellent view both up the Tista and the Talung. In order to get this view though it has been built

---

16 Corn.

a few feet above the road and it was this last steep climb which made us both weary to the extreme. The march had taken less than eight hours but I retired to lie on the floor for ten minutes or so on arrival before I was able to do much constructive. Though we did not realise it at the time we had climbed about 3,500 ft over some horrible tracks during a very hot day; it was not surprising that we were tired and very shortly stiff. At the time we were rather disappointed about it. We lazed around for the rest of the afternoon but found it rather chill for sitting outside. These days followed standard pattern of weather with a bright morning followed in due course by clouds from the South which by two o'clock had made the whole sky overcast; sometime before dusk the wind changed to the North and it blew the cloud back to the plains. This should have made it cool in the afternoons but it did not turn about early enough to have much effect on us as we reckoned to be in the bungalow by three at the latest.

The coolies this night were very late in arriving, coming long after dark and even then the sirdar had to go down to fetch them. The story we were told was that one of them had lost his kit down the khud-side and they had all stopped to collect it. This struck us as most unlikely and to judge from later experience I think that they had stopped off for a not so quick one at the many drink stops on the route.

It was not sufficiently cold at this stage to have fire and having nothing especially to tempt us otherwise we went to bed very early. We had brought an excess of kit with us – though in the event we used only a portion of the clothing – and at this stage we changed religiously into pyjamas every night. With these sweaty days the evening bath was high on the list of priorities, a place it was soon to lose.

Saturday October 7th. This was another day of sheer hard work. We were not in the mountains but merely a place where it was difficult to move about. The mountains proper were still hiding behind the wooded foot hills and all we were able to see were great tree-clad slopes leading up to sharp vegetated summits. They are not an inspiring sight when one is toiling along in the bottom of a gorge. The impression one gets is that the whole thing is never ending. Even on the best of level track we did not seem to pass the mileposts at more than two an hour. That, and the fact that a place on the opposite side of the valley at your own level might be more than a day's journey away I found rather depressing. One has only the hope of better things to come to keep one going.

The stage from Singhik to Chungthang is twelve miles with a net climb of under 1,000 ft. It sounds too easy but we took our full time over it, and arrived as tired as usual. The first half is a seven mile walk along the south side of the river as far as the bridge at Toong. There is a bungalow at this point which we used on the way back but its object is not very apparent. This part of the road is downhill on balance but spends so much of its time going up and down that that does not really affect the issue. At about half past ten we came down the final steep corner to the river where there was a gang of labour engaged in putting up a new wooden bridge. To judge by the area of rock washed clean by the river, the Tista had really gone to town at this point. The river is not very wide here and it must have risen a long way. They were making a wooden bridge and they had the two supports built out to within twenty feet of each other. In a day or two the thing would be ready. Meantime there was a cane bridge in action. CBS crossed first and did not approve of the idea at all, but I must say that I rather enjoyed it. It was at least exhilarating to be suspended so flimsily above the river. Just beyond the bridge I distinguished myself by hoofing it into a quicksand twice running on my way to and from a drink.

We had spent some time at the bridge and so we decided to lunch a little way on. We climbed cheerfully enough up through the forest to a spot where we hoped that there were no leeches and settled down to eat our dates and biscuits. The road before Toong was alleged to be 'accha'[17] but just before the bungalow we crossed one large and one small slide. These were our first experience of crossing rather than circumventing the slips and, though they were both old slides, and probably as safe as any, we neither of us enjoyed the process, the slip continuing below us for several hundred feet straight to the river, The road from Toong to Chungthang was said to be bahut kharaband[18] and we were more than anxious to find out what that implied.

Luckily for us the roads were classified on their ability to take loaded men or mules and for them the standard necessary is very different than that desirable for us who had only small packs on though they seemed to us to be horribly heavy. We did not mind delicate stuff over which a laden man could not pass. In a short way from the bridge the river turns due north again and the road follows it a hundred feet or so above. On this section two slides had occurred both of which we attacked by the direct route across as we were upon them before we had seen any diversion. This process is really very dangerous as the slips are by no means stable and most of the holds are mere boulders lodged in the moraine. But standards of safety in such matters are rather lower in this part of the world than say in the Alps where slips are a rarity. If it were not so one would never be able to move around. Anyway we ourselves got across both without any damage or even a scare. The next section wanders up the hill through what passes for a village, presumably taking this course because the original path by the river was washed away some time ago.

The villages at this level are not close groups of houses like an Alpine village but a series of shacks scattered over the cultivated area. This cultivation is mainly of rice and suchlike things, grass being considered unworthy of attention. There are very few animals to be seen though I presume they keep a number of cows somewhere. After this small section of cultivation the track returns to near river level and there was a third slip. This one was quite impossible to cross as it had been stripped down to the bare rock. So we cast back for the diversion and found a jungly one which climbed up creepers and down tree trunks without much compunction. This, like the bridge, rather woke the party up and though it consumed a lot of energy speeded later progress. At the other side we stopped to have the remains of the food, but it was not a cheerful spot as there were a number of leeches around and we had to sit in the middle of the road to get away from them.

From here on is a bit of good road which winds up and we yelled for the chowkidar with no result and in desperation set out for the village passing on the way the Post Office and the Police Outpost both of which were completely devoid of life. These two buildings are near the bungalow and separated from the village by a stretch of grass which might almost be called a meadow, though at this time of year it was hay on end.

The chowkidar was found in his house and alleged that his son was at the bungalow keeping watch with the key. He was at the bungalow but sound asleep. This man was one of those who live on dry rice and water and had absolutely nothing to offer. He had the excuse that most of the stuff had been sent up to Lachung as an emergency relief measure. As a result we rashly tried to make some soup from soup powder with hot water only and without boiling it. This was a ghastly failure, the product not only tasting grim but most of it was left in the cup as a sludge. It was cold this

---

17 Good.

18 Lots of money.

evening and we called for a fire as soon as the sirdar had arrived. The coolies were again late but not as bad as they had no excuse as although we ourselves did not use the diversions there was one at every slip and they were quite easy even for laden men.

Sunday October 8th. We got away to another early start on what we thought would probably be the hardest day of the lot. The road was definitely stated to be in a bad way and the stage itself was some ten miles long with a net climb of 2,500 ft. We started off on the wrong foot as within half a mile of the bungalow there was a slip which had to be avoided and we took a path straight up the hill. It went on and on and as we had not taken any note of how large the slip was, we over-shot. Luckily for us we met a local who took us back and showed us the correct track. This was rather an apology for a path but did after crossing much horrid ground come out on the road. We found the sirdar already there having come up by the river bed. We cursed loudly that he had not seen fit to tell us all about it. It was at all times very difficult to get from anyone any intelligible information as to the precise route to be taken or the state of the road at any given point. They seemed neither to know much nor to be able to explain that which they did know. This side of the hill is not heavily wooded although it faces due south – in fact there is quite a lot of outcropping rock though most of the surface is scrub. The road then continues in a sober fashion for some way with minor deviations where someone's fields have been washed away. We found it very difficult to pick up the diversion on these occasions as it did not appear to have been used much and certainly not by anything heavier than a human. As we were coming parallel to the village of Kedum which is on the south bank – and which the map showed to be only a very short way from Chunathang – the path forked and we had no idea of what to do. Village is rather flattery for Kedum as it is more truly the name of the fields which grow the fodder which is stored in the shacks which might be said to constitute a village. The lower path looked the more used and so after a brief halt – and the removal of the last leech of the season – we went down that. But in a very few yards we both stopped and protested at the loss of height, the river at this point a long 500 ft below and did not seem a good target. It was not a difficult decision and we were soon back on the other path making good progress through grass which was often knee high. We were not too discouraged though, as the path had obviously been used recently although it seemed as though it had been previously 'band' for a long time. There were a number of minor obstacles like tree trunks to be overcome until we came to a vast land slip across which there was no hope of progress. We cast back for the diversion but without success and so started out on what was fairly obviously a false trail though leading in the right direction. As, about ten minutes before, we had met a party of girls going the other way we were sure that there must be a way somewhere. This jungle bashing is not to my taste and became even less so when my eye was nearly poked out by an aggressive branch in the seven foot high scrub.

We tired rapidly of this ploy and when we sat down to consider things almost immediately heard voices which quickly materialized into yet another party of girls going down a track about six feet away. Our luck was definitely in and we quickly got back on to the track which was very jungly indeed. It was so bad in fact, that I was both swearing and sweating freely at it and the sundry things which tripped me up before we had even gone 100 yds. It had a delightful habit of approaching the side of the slip to within three feet, allowing to catch a glimpse of the depths below and then shearing away again in fright. When it recovered from the slip the path did not get back to normal, being apparently a diversion made many years before for some other slip. This was all right for a bit but then it started climbing up rocks on bits of wood which looked most rotten but never gave way in the event. These pieces of wood are dug into crevices and lashed to tree trunks to give the appearance of complete unreliability. The joys wound up by the crossing by a direct route of one vast and old slip. Then we got back to a decent path and having made virtually no progress in the previous half hour, we happened on a traveller who offered us some of the famous Lachung apples so we stopped to review the situation.

This man alleged that the path from here on was in good order and for once he was telling the truth. After exchanging one of CBS's cigarettes for a further supply of apples we walked on and made good progress into a more civilised part of the world. The river had now come out of its gorge and on our side there was a ledge of fairly flat land which was cultivated. These fields were dotted with the local version of the chalet which had no living accommodation. Most of them looked in bad condition and the fields deserted, the bhuttas which were the main crop being now nothing more than gaunt stalks.

The valley at this stage turns from E-W to N-S and the view to the north opens out to give some stimulating views of mountains although they are all described as 'sab se chota walla' mountains. That is the standard answer if they do not know the name of the mountain or if it had none. There seems to be a great shortage of names in this part of the world although I imagine that the yakherds must have more detailed names for everything. While we were lying in the middle of the path drinking from a small stream which crossed it we were approached by a family who gave us a couple of bhuttas as well as the usual apples. This was the only occasion on which we were given anything as a friendly gesture and the normal form of greeting at this level and below was a loud yell for baksheesh. This latter used to annoy me greatly as it brought one back so sharply to the streets of Calcutta. The last section of the road into Lachung has been washed away and the route lies along the river bed as usual over hung by large moraines. Mr Bercy Brown says that the village is first glimpsed from so many miles away nestling between the two rivers. To be more accurate it lies on the north end of the cone of debris brought down by the tributary and is set in a bare and mournful pasture. Of course the whole scene is now dominated by the fact that the middle of the valley is a 300 yd wide desolation where the river used to be only 20 yds or so. About a third of the village went down on September 14th, that is about 38 houses, and 18 people were killed in the village as well as a number of Tibetans who were camped by the river further up the valley. It really is a most impressive demonstration of the power of the river as some of the boulders which were brought down were of an immense size, and all the damage was done within half an hour. The dak bungalow which lies on the opposite side of the river to the village narrowly escaped as the water came to within 20 yds of the front door. The most vital out-buildings had been washed away. We thought of putting a note in the book suggesting that the PRD treat this as a number one priority.

We found the bungalow swarming with people and soon gathered that the Maharajkumar was expected that night. He had been on a tour of the Sebu Lakes to see for himself where the flood started, and was now on his way back to Gangtok. He had followed the Dewan over from Yatung but was going back by the normal route down the valley. Our arrival put a big spoke in the wheel as he was planned to occupy one half of the bungalow and the more important members of his staff the other. The chowkidar flapped hard.

It was all too easily solved as the reception committee which met him invited him over to the village and he crossed over as soon as he had arrived. This reception committee was a gorgeous show. The Lamas from the monastery laid on a band which led the procession making an outrageous noise, while Himself followed on behind chewing an apple. All the worthies of Lachung then presented their salaams and talked for a few minutes. Then the whole show dissolved, the Lamas getting a word of thanks for their efforts while the dignitaries faded into the background and Himself grabbed his staff and padded off to the village in his gym-shoes.

We had a look at the village which is more like an Alpine village than any had been so far. The houses are all built crowded on top of one another. The basement is of masonry in which the farm products are stored and in the wooden top everybody lives. The windows are the vehicle for such art as goes into their construction and the frames are carved to extremely complicated geometrical shapes and painted in gorgeous bright colours. All the houses are built to the same design and I presume that the carved window is the drawing room one. In between the houses are masses of apple trees which were just now dropping their fruit. The apples are not really Grade A unless they are eaten in great hunger. They are a good cooking apple but too large and coarse for an eater. Nevertheless we did eat large numbers of them. They also grow beans and potatoes on a large scale and we stocked up with these vegetables at this point. Also we bought some cabbages which got too near the paraffin somewhere on the march and were not so good thereafter.

Though we were deprived of the company of the Rajkumar we had a host of his minions in attendance, a long time listening to some of the woes and worries of the SDO. He seemed to be only interested in roads and such like and not in legal activities. He was planning to make the road from Chungthang cross the river at Kedum and go up the left bank past the bad slips and then back on to the intact portion. It struck us that it would cost a lot of money for so small a place. Lachung is at 8,500 ft and is cold in the evening so we got as close as possible to the fire which had been prepared for the Maharajkumar and hoped that we were to get it free. Even if we did that, the chowkidar got his own back by the chicken which he sold us. It was the toughest thing for miles around and defeated even our appetites. The old rogue must have bought the most ancient bird in the village especially for the use of travellers and what really hurt was that he charged Rs5 for it and we had agreed to pay before we sunk our teeth in it or rather before we had tried to sink our teeth in it.

Monday October 9th. Today was quite a short one being only ten miles and 3500 ft and we were getting in to trim. The road was alleged to be very bad but it was not said with quite the same conviction as further down the valley. The valley at this stage has opened out a lot and life is much easier for the traveller. All the same we decided an early start was a good thing although the locals seeing us set off seemed to think that we must be on our way to Mome Samdong in one. That however was more than we could contemplate.

The route started off along the river in the best style through what remained of the 'State ke Apple Garden' in which the bungalow and its vital outbuilding used to stand. The mountains on either side though only 16,000 ft or so had touches of snow on their north sides and jagged rocky crests rather than the smoother outlines of the lower hills. This is the stage one begins to ask excitedly what the name of a mountain is and is told that it is beneath contempt. Otherwise the road is dull, wandering inconsequently about through rhododendron scrub or more open country or through pine woods. Some of the slips in the river are most spectacular to look at but it is nearly always easy to get round them. At one point, we crossed a great plain of sand washed down by the river which was at least a quarter of a mile in length with a few gaunt trees standing in the middle. The river at this point was crossed and recrossed by the most kutcha but serviceable of bridges. They really get to work quickly on such things in this part of the world. Admittedly this is the trade route to the Donkya La but I do not imagine that much ever goes down this valley as the pass at the head of the Lachen valley is very much lower and the path better throughout. Be that as it may there were mule tracks on the Lachung Yeumthang section though we did not see any in action. At about lunch time we met a group of three working on the road – they were sitting down beside it but that is characteristic of those who work on the road. They all have a peculiar milk smell which is not unpleasant and I maintain that can often detect their presence better by the nose than by the eyes. Anyway I smelled these three before I saw them. They were most intrigued by the phenomenon of sahibs up a road in this state and one of them wanted to see my boots and try them on; though of course the boots did not make any attempt to fit over his vast Hillman's ankles. These people were on the Tibetan diet and were mixing themselves tea and tsampa[19] into a paste which was kneaded into balls and thrown deftly down the throat. The Dewan was saying that the people of this part of the world were keener on getting their flood relief in the form of tsampa from Tibet than as rice from India as the latter was such a prodigious price.

Yeumthang is prettily situated on the west side of the plain of that name. This is not really a plain at all but is a broad open space in the pine forests in which there is some pasture for the yaks and a number of huts for the yakherds. As a result of the flood the centre of the valley is now one broad scar strewn with wood and trees where before there must have been only a small river in a broad meadow. One is at 12,000 ft here and though it was not a subject of conversation between us we both had the slightest touches of mountain sickness. A well organised party would rest a day here to acclimatise but we were far too impatient for that sort of thing. As usual we arrived before two and found no chowkidar. He at length appeared from the river carrying a mass of wood. It was like an ice-house in the bungalow and we demanded a fire. He laid on the new wood from the river, but when it was pointed out to him that it did not burn he produced some magnificent logs which went up in a sheet of flame. Even so after the necessary cup of tea I decided that the bungalow was far too cold for spending the rest of the afternoon in and popped out for some exercise, leaving CBS giving himself chilblains over the fire – or rather, he should have given himself chilblains if he was liable to the things.

I first went down and inspected the yaks which were the first ones I had seen outside the zoo. There were five scattered round the meadow; from the front they were lovely soft faced creatures rather like a Channel Island cow gone the wrong colour whereas from behind they were too preposterous for words as they have a tail which obviously belongs to another animal. These beasts had lovely glossy coats hanging right down to the ground beneath but quite short on top. After deciding that yaks were attractive animals I walked up through the pine wood just to the north of the bungalow and out on to the old scree at the top. Here the scrub had grown to about four feet high except where a stream has washed out recently and had left a nice pathway. The bushes were filled with countless birds. I was not able to recognise any of them for certain but only to place them in their classes. In the low jungle it is very difficult to see the birds, of which there are a large number, without stopping and searching thoroughly. At the pine wood level it is easier but we were then more usually interested in making progress than in bird watching. Out beyond the tree line, though the birds are fewer its easy to see them if not to identify them.

I sat down and surveyed the scene looking across the valley to the first of the glaciers and up the valley to a peak of permanent snow which appeared to block it. Up here one was really in the mountains and no nonsense; indeed at this point I was higher than I had ever been before. I

19 Roasted flour, sometimes mixed with buttery tea.

must have felt that I was in the mountains to go for an evening walk. Coming down from my perch I crossed the river by a fallen tree trunk and wandered up across a vast expanse of rack and sand which had been brought down in the flood. From the top of this desert, which is the best part of a mile long, one can see the Burum La a 16,000 ft pass over to the Lachen Valley. It is seldom used by tourists as it is rather pointless. Just below the pass are some lakes which the Maharajkumar had visited a couple of days before. One could also see from the top end of the waste that the mountain which had appeared to block the valley was actually on the left hand side and the main river went up through a wide swath of debris between thick pine woods. The original path of which little was left had crossed the river just above the bungalow and then crossed back nearly half way to Mome Samdong. The kutcha bridge was a replacement and not just an accidental tree trunk which it appeared to be.

Back at the bungalow CBS laughed heartily when I said that I had been out for some 'exercise' while he had spent a lot of energy in getting close enough to the fire to remain warm. That night was truly cold though naturally not as cold as some that were to come.

Tuesday October 10th. This morning the ground was covered with frost and there was no tendency to spring out of the sleeping bag in the morning. CBS retreated into longs at this stage but I remained in shorts for one further day although they were reinforced with a sweater worn all day. Our reports as to the road were vague in the extreme but it was apparently open to ponies although we had been told the contrary only the day before. If there were some pony tracks it should be easy enough to follow the path.

At this stage we had the two tents put up in the bungalow area to see that everything was OK and luckily it was. Ours was a very smart affair with a sewn in ground sheet and openings at both ends. These were circular and could be drawn together and tied up from either side. In addition, there were two ventilation holes but for the first few days we apparently failed to get these latter properly adjusted and suffered accordingly. The coolies had a much larger but being without the special amenities of ours it must have been a draughty place at the best of times though they made no loud complaints about it and so I suppose that it was a standard issue.

The first half hour of the route I had done the day before and the following section was relatively intact as it wandered along the left bank of the river well about the damage line. The track crossed back to the right bank at about the tree line and climbed steeply for a little way. There was then a considerable portion which had been washed away and the diversion climbed steeply up the khud-side into the region of the rhododendron and azalea scrub. For some way we were able to follow the track easily enough as it had been made by many ponies but in a bit it ran out on some hard ground where their hoofs had made little impression. There we saw a path going up the hill to the left, which hillside was scree for a 1000 ft giving way to some rather delicious cliffs. Not imagining that there could be two paths in this place we took the left hand course and climbed up into the higher regions only to be left stranded 500 ft higher with no path to follow. From this height it was obvious that there was no major slip for which this might be the diversion and so we were altogether foxed. So we sat down and had our lunch and while we were eating we saw the sirdar and one coolie coming up from below. We sat and watched their progress and noted that they went straight up along the river although there was no very evident path there. Our course was obvious and we started off diagonally down the hill but got involved in no time with a thigh high scrub which was very hard work; as well as being bad for bare legs– the protective layer of dirt and sun-burn was removed in no time. At this point we gave up and turned straight down the hill and hoped to get out into the open as soon as could be. We rolled and tumbled down as best we might. Luckily ever since Singhik we had been removing stuff from our packs as we had found them much too heavy and now carried only the vital things. If we had heavy packs, the easiest way would have been to fall down. At the bottom we found some signs of a track which wandered along the margin of the river. The sirdar and the coolie were now some way ahead

We followed up and found them sitting on the path and haggling with a mule driver for a piece of yak cheese which looked more like a bad haggis than anything else. This stuff went into their curry for many days to come. Cigarettes seem to be the main currency in these operations. We were both suffering from headaches and we sat down to let the sirdar overtake and lead the way. By now we were at the junction of the two rivers from the Sebu and Donkya Las and the way to the camp was alleged to lie up the right bank of the left hand branch. In fact it went most of the way over the boulders which the stream had brought down. The flood water in this part of the river must have moved at an enormous pace as whereas lower down the river had in places risen by 100 ft or so up here 20 ft was the normal maximum and the spread was not so great either. The sirdar went rapidly ahead of us, as we were making bad progress, and crossed the river at some place unknown. We followed up the bank and found no place which we thought worthy of being called a ford and the ponies left no tracks on the boulders. If there is one thing that I hate it is fording rivers when I am not feeling on the top of form and now I was very far from that state. I was mighty annoyed with Thandu for dashing on without telling the sahibs all about it. In the end we chose a place which was slightly better than the others and CPS jumped across quite successfully. My camera was handed over and then I jumped straight into the pani.[20] That was the bottom, I was now wet, cold and very irritated. We rushed off up to the hut where the two had succeeded in doing absolutely nothing whatever. Mome Samdong is built on the peninsula between the two rivers and slopes slightly less steeply than the rest of the the hill. Behind it is a great bare scree mountain which reminds one of some of the more desolate parts of the Highlands. To the west there are some quite steep mountains with a bit of snow on the top – though they are negotiable without much difficulty – and behind them are the things of 20,000 ft and more just south of the Sebu La. To the NE on the path to the Donkya La one can see the Donkya Rhee, a fine point of rock and snow which is not likely to be climbed by normal man. Pauhunri is just a bit further round to the right but is not so impressive.

To say that Mome Samdong is 'built' is a bit of an exaggeration as the buildings consist of one yakherd's hut with its prayer flags, a few shelters for yaks and the remains the Himalayan f hut. This was a fine building which stood four square to the south being built in the manner of many Alpine huts. Unfortunately the roof of tin sheets had been blown away and the lack of a lock on the door has left the interior in rather a shambles. However our coolies preferred to sleep in this draughty and smoke ridden spot rather than in their tent. All the food was cooked over a fire which, even though the original draught arrangements may have been good, is in its present state a perfect devil for smoke. We had most of our meals in there as it was so cold elsewhere but paid the price of sore eyes.

In not so long they had the tent up at a spot just behind the hut, and we piled in only to realise that we had no kit with us as the other coolies had not turned up. As luck would have it we had one blanket and four sheets – these latter were taken on the trip under somewhat of a

20 Water.

misapprehension – and these were hardly enough to keep out the cold from either of us. We sat there for about two hours being the very pictures of misery until at five or so the others deigned to roll in. We quickly crammed on the clothes and tried to forget how grim we were feeling.

This bad organisation was mostly in my opinion the sirdar's fault as he had instructions that all were to go together and he should have had the sense to bring some tea and flour with him so that we could have a bite to eat on arrival. He was all the way a bit disturbed by the fact that we went on ahead of himself and the coolies, arriving long before the scheduled hour. However, we liked travelling in the early morning and saw no reason why we should dawdle on the way if we could avoid it. That night was bad, but bad; we tried to take some whisky to cheer us up but could not manage it, and our meal went back mostly uneaten. We were cold most of the night and very restless with a slight headache all the time. One symptom of mountain sickness we did not have was a tendency to vomit so we were lucky in that measure.

Wednesday October 11th. In the morning we were not feeling by any means too good but being both inordinately obstinate we decided to go on as planned and make a reconnaissance in the direction of the Sebu La. Not unnaturally we wanted to take the sirdar with us to carry the food and generally act as a guide. This pained him somewhat and I was not able to find out why. I can only think that he did not consider it part of his job, but our ideas were very different. We started off a bit later than usual due to the extra time required for cooking the meals under camp conditions. The route is intact for the first mile or so along the north bank of the river up to the Sebu Lakes, then one comes to the hot springs which have been spared by the flood. Thandu here insisted on washing though we regarded it as far too cold. From here on, the path goes across the boulders brought down by the river to a nice cliff just to the right of the main stream. It is avoidable on the left by a considerable detour but it looked as though the direct route might be fun. Thandu obviously did not like the look of it but condescended to be directed up the obvious and easy if somewhat spectacular route. He –Thandu– liked it even less at the top and for one pitch took off his boots, a quite unnecessary operation. In fact I was thoroughly disappointed with his performance on this occasion. He obviously would not be much good in any place where really high class climbing was needed. Up at the top of this cliff is the remains of the first lake. This is now completely dry and has left a big mess. The route out on to the top level is to the right and is quite simple provided one knows where to go. The second lake is about twenty feet below its original level and had at this time got a few big bergs floating around in it. It was these which had caused the damage, having been part of an avalanche which fell from the glacier coming into the west side of the lake and set up such big waves that the moraine dams were broken.

Having got to the second lake, the path – or rather, the route for there is no path – takes to the hillside and goes up at a great rate to the upper basin. It was at this point that I completely gave out. It was a form of mountain sickness, which showed itself by a great shortage of breath. The height I suppose was 17,000 ft, which is not all that high but I was not able to make more than a hundred paces at a time. CBS was in rather better shape and could make about double the number. He claimed that he was fit to go on the top to which the sirdar said we could go and return in two hours. It was decided that I should stay where I was and they would go on. It was a very bad arrangement as I realised in those ten minutes when they were overdue, but as it happened all came right in the end. The pair of them got to the top and were greatly impressed by the view. I in my resort, though realising that the view was good was more impressed by the cold which was intense when the cloud finally came up to cover the sun.

On his return CBS was dead tired and I was again peeved with the sirdar for ever allowing him to get into such a state. Where the weather changes with such speed, one must be on the toes all the time. On this occasion the weather changed rather too quickly for our liking. Instead of there being mere clouds in the afternoon as was the usual they turned to snow despite the fact that Thandu said that there would be none. Luckily it did not snow hard or we would have had a job getting CBS back to camp. As it was Thandu showed a distinct tendency to wander on without orders to get himself back to the warm as soon as he could.

We avoided the cliff by going to the south of the river, and after an interminable time we got back to Mome. We were now ready to admit that we were not feeling too good. Our appetite dropped to the minimum that night, though with the snow actually falling it was not too cold for the empty stomachs. We spent an age in the hut trying to get comfortable despite the smoke and lack of leg room, but without any great success.

Thursday October 12th. We decided on a day off. We hoped that this might give us time to get over the worst effects. It was a pleasant morning without any of the snow left on the ground, and CBS availing himself of his ability to sleep in any occasion dozed off in the sun. Many good intentions floated through my mind but got no further. Indeed the furthest that I got was to a sunny sheltered spot behind a moraine hill about two hundred yards off. There I was quite content, until lunchtime. The afternoon was even more cloudy than most of them and consequently colder so we retired to bed or to a similar state of indifference.

Friday October 13th. This was to be the vital day as we were to go over the Donkya La which is over 18,000 ft and takes one over onto the Tibetan plateau though the place is politically still in Sikkim. It is a climb of just about 3,000 ft as well as a long way on the ground. There was a little snow on the floor and a lot of cloud in the air when we set off at eight o'clock. It goes without saying that we were carrying nothing except ourselves but we found that rather more strain than the coolies found in their loads. One thing that the Sherpas seem to hate is the cold, under the influence of which they will go like bombs. Certainly this day we were in no fit state to do more than barely hold our own. The road is nothing better than dull unless one can see all the mountains. We had a few glances of the Donkya Rhee and one or two of Pauhuri but not really enough to dispel the fumes of the headaches. After a long period of hard work beside the river the valley opens out into a drear plateau with the pass as a nick in the ridge due north. At about this stage we began to suffer from the breathlessness again, though not on the previous scale. As luck would have it after a quarter of an hour of this I got a second wind and by using my lungs like bellows I was able to keep up a cracking pace and catch up with the coolies again. These we left at the foot of the last 200 ft to the pass – where I took a picture of one of our Allsopps Lager vases for publicity purposes. The top is dramatic – one comes up from a country of sharp peaks and deep gorges and great snowfields and looks over on to the plateau which, as you might have guessed, is not really that flat. From a distance it looks rather like the Highlands in spring with the mountains just flecked with snow. All the hills appear to be of the same height and there is no question of identifying any particular one. We sat on the top and admired the view for some time though the coolies, feeling the cold, dashed straight over the top and down the other side. It was cold on top and the snow was only a little way behind us so there was no great inducement to dawdle on the way down. The main feature of the near landscape is Chho Llamo a great long lake nestling under a vast lump of brown hill. Our path lay over some large size scree and was not comfortable though it was used regularly by the yaks. To our left as we were going down was a spectacular ridge and glacier system though the glacier was not a very big one. I imagine that most of the monsoon gets stopped on the south side of the ridge. The river at the bottom flows into the Lachen Chu and the watershed dividing the Tista and the Nepal rivers is one further over to the north being in fact the political frontier. Though we had got over the worst of our headaches we were not feeling too strong and we went slowly and were left a long way behind the porters. They however had the sense to leave somebody to show us the way in though the man did not really know where the place was meant to be. Down in the plain there was a mighty cold gale blowing which made life a trifle bitter. The camp was just under the lee of a small ridge, facing north across the wide river bed to a brown hill which was the Tibetan border. The two tents had been pitched at what was to be their highest for the trip, being at about 17,000 ft. We crowded round the tea and revived rapidly though we never got to the stage of feeling chirpy that night. It snowed again which was a good thing from the point of view of keeping the temperature up but not so good for the next day's march. As we had a lot of time to spare the idea of dawdling across this part of the trek was in our minds as we would have liked to have had a general look around that part. 17,000 ft, however, is not the height to be at if the weather is not up to standard. We had decided that if it snowed in the night we would go on down to Dokyang and give the further exploration of Chho Lamo the miss. This would be a pity but a preferable alternative to being cold and miserable for days on end.

Saturday October 14th. There was an inch or two of snow on the floor, it was wet and there was a deal of cloud about. Indeed the whole prospect was dismal and we decided on a speedy retreat. Climbing the odd 100 ft on to the broad ridge behind the camp we then went over to the river finding that though the retreat was easy the speedy part was not. The river coming out of Chho Llamo is more of a swamp than anything else and was covered with ice. No one fell in so that was the first obstacle met. The next one was the snow which was just deep enough to be a nuisance and not deep enough to be a pest. There were two theories of progress, the up and the down, i.e. along the side of the hill or down in the valley and the better was the one which did not happen to be up to its knees in snow. After a bit of this sort of thing the sun arrived and the whole world came to life although the mountains, which are supposed to be especially beautiful at this point, were still in cloud. The Dewan had a very good selection of pictures of this area taken when he was up there in May. We stopped at Gurongolmar for so called lunch and there we saw the last of the sirdar for the day. He apparently decided that it was going to snow and that he was better out of it, so he walked ahead and be took himself to the yakherd's hut at Dokyang. What he forgot though was that none of the coolies knew the route well although some of them had been over it before. Luckily for us we walked on more or less with the coolies and so were with them when the weather broke.

But before then we had a pleasant walk along the south side of the valley which here runs more or less due EW. At one time we saw an enormous herd of yak away on the far side of the valley; there must have been fully 200 of them. We passed a number of shelters for the yakherds but none of them were then in use. There was a very strong wind blowing most of the time and when the valley turned south to go down to Dokyang the wind began to bring some sleet with it. At first we did not take this very seriously and I foolishly did not bother to cover up my face, for which omission I was to suffer. As we got right into the mouth of the valley the going changed from bare rocky yak pasture to shallow snow and at the time the cloud come down and visibility was only a few hundred yards. I imagine that the foul weather had been blowing up the valley most of the day and it was us that walked into it rather than the other way about.

It was about at this stage that we began to ask the coolies where the camping place was. At first we got confident replies that it was only a little further and that they knew all about it. A little later, they did not claim to know quite so much about it, but were certain that the right place was only a little further down the valley. CBS was beginning to have doubts as to whether the chaps had a clue where they were. The country was rather like the most desolate parts of the Pennines at the dead of winter, quite featureless with the present amount of cloud about. This suspense went on for some time and then we came to the conclusion that action was necessary – the coolies were obviously tiring and going against the wind and sleet would put an end to them in no time. So at half past four we decided to camp and after a small amount of flap found a place facing north in the lee of a large drift where we thought the wind would not be so bad. The porters at this stage were announcing that they were going to die and such like stuff. One of them complaining loudly saw a pile of stones on the other side of the river and announced that he was going there. He was such a pest that I let him go though I did not think that we should see him again that night if at all. The rest of them were made snug in the tent although needed a lot of encouragement to do anything whatever. After tea they announced that they could not have anything to eat as one cannot cook rice in snow. That was soon disproved though I would admit that their method does not produce good results under these conditions. We were thankful that we had brought the primus – it was the only night on which it was the only form of fire available. It gave out last thing at night but was revived in time to produce the morning cup of tea. Our tent was pitched just to the lee of the big one and so should been out of the wind. But it was very definitely in the snow and we had the most uncomfortable of nights. I suppose as we walked quite a distance the next day, we must have had some sleep, though it did not seem so at the time. We were rolling this way and that in an attempt to keep warm and get the bumps out of the back. A very definitely miserable night.

Sunday October 15th. We were glad to hear the tea arriving in the morning but not so glad to hear the sirdar. Here poured forth a long stream of excuses virtually saying that it was all our fault and that he was a magnificent fellow, and not explaining that when one of the coolies had reached Dokyang the night before he had not come back and looked to his duty. We thought of a number of awful punishments, none of which were carried into effect. Instead we maintained a supposedly stern silence and demanded that breakfast be brought soon.

The morning was fine and the whole place being snow looked most pleasant in the sunlight. We saw then that the target was just on the other side of the river, though to get to it one had to go a mile or more down river and up again. Behind us there was a steep mountain rising right up to 19,000 ft or so and very impressive snow clad in the morning sun. Though we were able to have our breakfast, the coolies' could not be cooked and they went off to Dokyang to get it organised there. This meant that we were sitting near the bridge over the river only too literally cooling our heels for a long time. Even though the sun was bright it was not hot. Up to this bridge we had been forging a new track through the snow and it had been hard work but from here on the track had been used that morning and was easy going. This path anyway is the main trade route and is kept in good order. The way meanders down the valley on the right bank all the way and is a sheer delight. The mountains were all deep in snow and glittering in the sun showing off all their best points. It was rather a strain on the eyes even in goggles.

At one time we had intended to stay at Dokyang and if it had not been such an unpleasant night we undoubtedly would have done so, though with so much snow we would not have made much progress in our explorations. But when one is feeling annoyed in the first place and cold in the second it is difficult to keep the temptation of the dak bungalow away. About twelve o'clock it clouded over as usual in this first half of the trip. The lower part of the valley is rather narrow, and not so pleasant as the open wastes above. It sounds blasé but we felt that we were getting very low when we came down to Thangu at 12,500 ft. The trees in this valley did not come much above the 13,00 ft mark though above that there was the usual scrub. The bungalow is well above the valley on the left bank and overlooks a wide stretch of wooded valley towards Lachen.

Snow was lying at this height. The bungalow was not snow bound though and showed signs of great activity. Indeed when we got there we found that Murray and Marshall were in occupation. As it happened neither party had passes for this day as they had overstayed by one day and we were early by the best part of ten. They had intended to spend two days there and then go over the Lungnak La but had been put off by the morning weather as they had not seen the first sun which we had enjoyed. Marshall was not quite up to scratch as he had blistered badly on the way up but he was not in such a bad way as myself, my lips having swollen to twice the normal size as a result of the wind of the day before. As usual we had arrived early though this time with the porters, but there was no question of devoting the day to anything other than rest and recuperation. Rashly I said that I would have a bath and greatly regretted it when I was frantically dashing the half inch of tepid water, over myself in an attempt to keep warm. The weather was going its usual was of turning to cloud in the afternoon but again I am glad to say it refrained from snowing.

We spent a lot of time being amazed at the amount of kit that the others were taking with them. They had thirteen porters altogether at this stage of which eleven were Sherpas. These included one each for themselves and one for the sirdar as well as a table boy though he carried something as well. When we saw them going off they were very lightly loaded which even the sirdar admitted. They had oodles of everything including a whole battery of cameras, which were strung around them. Though admittedly it was sheer chance that it happened to them, their party ended in a bad way, despite all the equipment. They went up to Goma and had to send one man down from there who we saw in Lachen sick of some mysterious disease. They spent three days up at Goma and found that they had another man sick and Marshall was still not really fit, so they decided to evacuate three days early and down the Lhonak Chu. One would have thought that the sirdars would have known how bad the road was and in fact they spent two days on the first four and a half miles. At that point two of his men could no longer walk and they had no porter who was really capable of carrying them; so they left them under a blanket under a rock beside the Lhonak Chu. Meanwhile the rest of the party did one march to Lachen in 19 hours arriving at five in the morning to send some of the locals back to fetch them. They found that one man was already dead and the other dying and for some unexplained reason they left them there. It all seems just unfortunate and not careless – the disease is so far unknown but must have been swift in action at this height.

Monday October 16th. The morning was not too bad and the others got away to a late start at about eight o'clock for no reason that we could see. It was said that it was impossible to cross the pass in one and so they were going to Pogi only, which is up at the top of the side valley and about five miles and 1500 ft from the bungalow. We did not feel like going on that day or for that matter going over the pass 'ek sath'[21] so we had another day of peace.

The state we were in can be seen from the fact that we did not go outside the bungalow all day, contenting ourselves with sitting over the fire and lapping up the literature which was

21 Together.

around. A large item in this was the bungalow book itself which contained excitements like the Everest expeditions and a number of other well known names. For me the other main item was the *Geographical Journal* and at the time I resolved to read it regularly but it takes on a different aspect in Calcutta. Both the nights we spent at Thangu were exceedingly cold despite the fires in the bungalow and on the second one at least when there was no nonsense about baths, there was no nonsense either about undressing. In the camp we had the art of dressing and undressing absolutely taped and the very minimum of time was so spent. Actually the names are rather the wrong way about as in the evening the plan was to take off the boots and put on sweaters enough to meet the conditions or all of them whichever was the larger and crawl into the sleeping bag sometimes forgetting to take off the hat; whereas in the morning the idea was to take off the pullovers and put on some shoes and the hat, if it had come off in the night, and sally forth.

Tuesday October 17th. The morning was again fine and the snow was thawing rapidly so there was no possible excuse for not moving. We had no plans for this part of the journey but there did not seem to be much alternative to going over the Lungnak La though this was not specifically mentioned in our permission to trek. We hoped that the authorities were not so efficient as to check on our movements. Once over, we again had not much idea but we were attracted by a path mentioned on the map as leading over the southern shoulder of a 19,000 ft peak by the name of Rokcha. This led over from the valley of the Chakla Chu back to the Lhonak Chu near Langpo. From thence we thought that we would go back over the The La because two of the porters claimed to know that route whereas no one had a clue about the Lhonak Chu which was the other obvious route back. And it was lucky that we did not try and get down by that route. Wherever we were going in the end we had the first two days over the Lungnak and back down to Mugotang on the Chakla Chu. The use of names in Lhonak does not imply that there is anybody there or that there ever has been. There is no permanent population of Lhomak but the herds of yak come in from Sikkim and Tibet in the cold and hot weathers when the men put up their houses of skin in the various localities where there are permanent foundations ready and these are the named places.

The first bit of the road along the Tibet route was encumbered by three teams of eight men each carrying great logs of pine up into Tibet for building bridges. These must be very expensive as the chaps get Rs2-8-0 a day for it. Where the road crosses over to the right bank of the river the path strikes off up a shoulder. It is not a broad mule track or anything as luxurious as that but is a comfortable enough path for the unladen man. The valley up which the track goes is only a small and narrow one and there is no cultivation in it and so the path keeps well up the north side, pleasantly in the sun. Pogi was our target for the day and lies up at the top of this stretch where the valley is closed by a steep rise. There is a supply of fuel at this point and some admirable rocks under which to light the fire. The trouble is that the tent 'jagah' is quite blocked as to air flow by these rocks which form an admirable frost pocket on a cold night. It was a cold night.

It was a very short day to get up here and so after a cup of tea I went on for a bit. With all the snow about there was not much alternative to going straight up the track to the pass as in any other direction I should have been tired out before I had climbed 1,000 ft. The first bit was pleasant going up the steep brow of the hill – about 600 ft – on a well beaten track. Above this although the track was well beaten it was not such steady going and one started to slip around a lot. I went on until I thought that I was only 200 ft from the top though the next day I saw that it was more nearly 500 ft. By this time I was distinctly tired and the clouds were doing their usual stunts. I thought that prudence demanded an about turn. Even going down through this stuff was not easy and I was crying out for tea when I got down to camp just after four. It was already cold as the sun had been off the camp for a long time. It steadily became colder all night and sleep was at a premium.

Wednesday October 18th. As a result of the cold we were a bit late in starting which was a pity as we knew that the going would be hard even with the track already made for us. The previous day on arrival at Pogi I had been pressing for an immediate start and over the pass in one day which only goes to show how silly one can be. The mountains in this part of the world were not spectacular perhaps because they had the rocks covered in a heavy layer of new snow. They go up to 17,000 ft and some of them would be very difficult to climb even from the 16,350 ft pass, and for some reason I have an enormous desire to try. The way up to the top was more hard work and unremitting. We went slower than I had the day before but even then on the top few hundred feet I found myself stopping regularly to recover energy. The view from the top was superb, the pass itself facing more or less north and looking across the head of the valley which comes up from Lhonak. I have no idea what the normal route down is but at the moment the trail went straight down an immensely steep slope of snow to tail off on to a plateau. This was all very hard going for the chaps and it was difficult enough for us to keep upright and going in the right direction. It was distinctly chilly on the top and we began the slow descent without delay except to take a picture of a porter attempting the shute – which did not come out.

At the bottom of this steep gully the trail led round to the right over rocks and snow which were most treacherous being designed to twist the ankles, and then down to the more or less level valley. Here we waited for the porters just above a small artificial lake. I imagine that in the hot weather water is scarce in the valleys without a glacier stream and these lakes have been built for the yaks though one would have thought that if water is so scarce the pasture cannot be up to much. The porters took less time than we thought they would and appeared not the least damaged though we had seen them sit down hard many times on the way down. From this point on the path wanders down the valley keeping mainly to the right bank. Some very little way on, at a point some five hours march from our start, we saw large camping rock where the others had spent the night. They must have got away to a very slow start not to have got further than this in one day. In one hour more we arrived at our camping place which was one of the most delightful spots we ever stopped at. It was well below the snow line, just a few feet above the stream and set in a veritable bed of gentians of a lovely pale blue shade. These gentians were all over the valley at this point but nowhere more so than at the camp. Behind the camp was a bare and uninteresting mountain, to the west Mugotang in about a mile, and to the SW the whole range of Kanchenjunga. This evening they were clear and looked too marvellous though of course not so far in the skies as they do from Darjeeling. We were here at about 14,500 ft.

Naturally enough in this exciting spot I could not sit still after the first cup of tea and I had hopes of getting some excellent pictures not realising that the mountains of the Kanchenjuga range look best from here in the morning when the sun is on their eastern slopes. The original idea was to cross the Chakla Chu and climb over the bare shoulder of a hill to look down on the main Lhonak valley. The vital part of this plan was to cross the river and knowing my antipathy for such things I thought that there might be some difficulty. There was and I walked for a long way down beside the river without success. From Mugotang southwards the river is wide and smooth and not good for fording, but at Mugotang itself it can be made, which fact I discovered when it as already too late to carry out the original plan.

Having been foiled at the south end I turned about and followed the river up. The stream down from the Lungnak La has brought down in time – or its glacier has – an enormous amount of moraine which has nearly blocked the valley. Above this block the Chakla Chu flows through a wide grassy plain the best part of a mile long at the upper end of which is a similar barrier though this time of rock. I went round the north edge of the moraine and found that a fair track went north along the edge of the plain and would do well for the next day's route. The man actually placed the path on the other side of the valley but there was now no reason for us crossing first thing in the morning. From the side of the plain I went straight up the hill until I came to the edge above the camp and could look down on the tents and out to the Kanchenjunga range.

I buttoned up and sat there to wait for the sun set and was solaced in my waiting by a magnificent view of the Zemu peak. From anywhere in this valley one can see this peak and I took a number of pictures of it always to find that in another place a few miles further up the view was even better. Actually the sunset was not very good, though I did not wait till the end as it was cold and I was thirsty.

That night there was a fine supply of wood in the form of an evergreen scrub bush known to the Sherpas as 'shupra' or some such. This stuff goes up in a sheet of flame on being put on the fire. It grows up to about 16,000 ft in sheltered places in the Chakla Chu area. As a result of its generosity we had two fires and had dinner in out of doors comfort. From here on we made our evening meal out a habit, which postpones the cramps of tent life, when it is possible. Things seemed to be getting a bit more organised from this angle of comfort. The coolies knew how to deal with our bedding and what clothes we would want in the day and all round the admin. was improved. It may have been though that we were no longer feeling ill, as well as getting more accustomed to the life.

Thursday October 19th. It was a fine morning so we decided to go north up the Chakla Chu and put a camp at the foot of the pass which was alleged to lead over the south shoulder of the mountain Rokcha. From our camp we had seen the mountain though the way up to the pass was out of sight round a corner. We had no reason to suppose that it would be very difficult to find the route as one should be able to count the number of streams on the map and check them off against the water on the ground. It was not to be. We started off in fine style after taking the ritual photograph of Kanchenjunga. For this part of the journey we were definitely in charge as none of the porters had been here and, though neither had we, we had the map such as it was. It is more satisfactory to be one's own directing staff in these things as one cannot then be led up the pole by ill reports of the state of the road and such like misleading tricks of idle servants. One can however only do it in country which they do not know at all. Even in country which they do know it is useful to know it also as they have a habit of altering distances to suit their own ends. One of the things which they insist on doing, and which I found very infuriating, is giving distances in terms of miles, a unit which has no meaning whatsoever in this sort of country. When asked to give it in terms of hours they goggle at length and then give a figure which will occupy the rest of the day or all the morrow as the case may be. In most country they do not seem to have much idea of time and motion but just go on till it is dark. The locals always ask you the time when they are passing through; what good it does them I cannot think.

We started off in too fine style as we over shot. We came to a place, called Shitong Dok on the map, which is a mere yakherd's shelter and there sat down to review the situation. We could not make it out. Right opposite was a stream bed coming down from the mountain which should have been the one we were looking for by all calculations. Yet there was no water in it and it was meant to drain a large area. Again the map marked a big re-entrant and there was none. In addition the sirdar, when we said that that was the route, said he would not go and we foolishly believed him. As we discovered later it is very easy indeed and was the stream we were looking for. However this time we decided to go on though we could not make the ground ahead fit the map in any fashion.

Even if the ground did not agree with the map it agrees with the party. At the head of the valley was the 22,000 ft, peak of Chho Yummo. This is a fine twin peak which stands on the frontier and presents a very good face to this valley. It is quite impossible in most places but I think one could get up the ridge to the central col without much difficulty. From a camp there in decent snow conditions it would be possible to get to the top in one. I meant to have a closer look at this route but the weather and chance did not allow. On the right of the valley are a series of snow mountains of various heights and consistent beauty and grandeur. Though the left hand is much more brown and bare it was to us the more interesting as it was the direction in which we were to go. We pressed or with the sirdar on a recce and crossed what we later showed to be the stream which comes down from the Yalung Lake. At this point this spreads over a large plain. From a little hill on the far side we had a good prospect up the next mile of the valley. We could see that the valley forked at a place which would do as a camp site as it was sheltered and had water and wood. We decided on the left hand fork and passed orders back via the sirdar. We ourselves went on intending to stop at the stream junction and eat there. There was no path at this stage but the route was very easy indeed except that there were a number of springs which caused floods and marshes. We were soon faced with the problem of crossing the main stream which we liked as little as usual. In this case it was genuinely a bit worse as it was covered in ice. In the event neither of us got wet. Under a boulder on the far side we had some food and got inordinately cold in the process.

After lunch we pressed on up the valley to the left but kept high on its north side in an attempt to see round the core to the top of the valley where we still expected to see our pass. Actually this was out of the question as we were on the wrong mountain altogether having come further up the valley than we had imagined. Our chosen route was not a good one as it was over a large scree, but it did enable us to see a pass at the head of the valley which was obviously not fit for coolies without some reconnaissance. While we were sitting down and thinking about it all the porters came over the brow into the valley and following the centre made good progress. So we, from above, directed them into a pleasant spot at about 16,000 ft, just beneath a step in the valley. There was a lot of wood around and the place should be protected from the wind while water is only twenty yards away. In fact we were rather pleased with our efforts as sirdars.

We ourselves wanted to go on a bit and so we turned due north up the hill on whose flank we had seen sitting. In a few hundred feet this route took us to the edge of the upper basin. From here I was certain that our valley was the one marked as going up into the middle of Roka even though it was not quite the right shape. This upper basin we were in had a col to the north just opposite us and from there rose two easy ridges, the one going to the east to an outlier on the high side of 18,000 ft and the other going up the main mass of the mountain presumed to be Roka. CBS wanted to go and have a look at this col but in the event found while he was traversing semicircularly leftwards that the way was blocked by some large and unstable scree lying at a steep angle. I on the other hand turned right as I wanted to get a view over to the north and Chho Yummo. I crossed over a large amount of this plateau and then climbed up to the eastern tail of the ridge. The sun was still on duty but there was a powerful wind blowing up from the south which made life chilly. So I hustled round to the north side of the ridge and climbed up in the lee of the wind. I climbed for quite some time up this ridge and then came out on the top at a break in the gradient just below the outlying peak. I stayed there just long enough to take a few photographs and calculate that I was at about 18,000 ft before turning and going eastwards down to the main valley of the Chakla Chu. At this point this is a wide and uninteresting stretch of grass and moss leading up to the pass over into Tibet. There is, though, a rather intriguing bare mountain to be seen just to the north and a valley which curls round invitingly to the west. In fact my whole self said turn north and have a better look at this country but my watch was adamant that it was time to be going home. So I went. The route then dropped sharply down to the level of the lower valley and although I made an uncomfortable attempt to keep height along the side of this steep and gravelly hill I was eventually forced to follow suit and descend to the bottom. There is another yakherd's place in this part of the valley although at this time it is of course as deserted as all the rest. It was not such a good camping place as our own. By the time I had lost enough height to be on the valley floor it was time to climb again to get over into the camp valley. This latter valley is a couple of hundred feet above the level of the main stream. As I got over the brow into the valley and into sight of the camp the sun was setting, and it became rapidly cold. There were twenty more minutes to be done.

Tea that night was welcome indeed as I was tired after all this effort at a fair height and, it must be admitted, tired by the excitement of it all. The evening was a most perfect one as there was enough wood for a 'burra' fire outside. We were facing Lachsi which though an uninteresting mountain to look at during the day is a glorious sight with the sun setting on it. It was a moonlit night and the light passed from the mountain to the sky and back again, first the sun lit up the snow, then the light passed to the sky behind which gradually darkening from its glimmering pallid blue gave up first place to the cold moonlit snow of the high places. Meantime we had had a good deal to eat though not quite enough. While we did not realise it at the time, when we were in Lhonak our appetites were building up and never being satisfied. In another day or two we suddenly realised what was going on and then there was no stopping until ten days or so after we had arrived back in Calcutta. The great appetite was partly due to the extra work we had being putting in and partly due to the absence of any trace of sickness, indeed to the presence of a burning fitness.

Friday October 20th. Appropriately enough being my birthday this was one of the most successful days of the whole trip. It was not distinguished by particularly fine weather, although there was nothing to complain about. The plan was that we two and the sirdar as 'guide' should go off for the day, although the sirdar knew less than nothing about the place. We thought that we would be able to get to the pass at the head of the valley and possibly have a crack at one of the hills on either side.

We started off in good order and followed a route which I had mapped out the previous day, although there was no great virtue in it. The rock on the north of the route could be climbed in a number of places but none of them appear to have the makings of a good pass. On the south of the valley the side would be a bit more difficult to climb though it could be done I am sure. We really should have tried the south with the porters though I think that we might have had difficulty getting down the other side. The problem was that the coolies and the sirdar did not relish the idea of going off the beaten and on that sort of thing co-operation and enthusiasms are essentials.

We climbed up small moraines and stream beds for about 1,500 ft until we came out in the upper basin which is a shambles of large moraines surrounded by steep walls. We crossed to the right under the valley head and made our way up in the shadow of the boundary ridge over the rubble of a recent rock fall. All the blocks of the moraine were very large and many of them equally unstable, though by keeping high we were able to get along in complete safety and great discomfort. This route ran out beneath the final pinnacle and a walk round that and we were on Thandu La[22] as we named it. I estimate that it is about 18,300 ft, and I am certain that it is not visited by the locals as there were no cairns around. On the left there is a gentle snow ridge leading up to the south peak of Roka while on the right hand there is a fearsome pinnacle of exceeding rotten rock. Before I saw it at close quarters I had made up my mind that it was to be climbed and named it the Meredith pinnacle but a nearer view unmade my mind at a great rate. Looking westwards there was a marvellous view of a snow and rock mountain which must have been on the right side of 20,000 ft. It could be climbed from this side without much difficulty. To its left there was a cirque of snow peaks all way up in the sky. They were a perfect selection and down from them came a series of large glaciers debauching into a small lake beneath the col right down in the valley. At this time the glaciers were covered in snow and few of the crevasses were showing though CBS was very impressed by the line of the ice-falls immediately opposite us. At this time of day the snow was in bad condition and progress through it would have been miserable. What little we tried put us off for a long time. One would have to be about it very early in the morning to make good going. To the north one could have a good view of Tibet while the river which drained the glaciers turned out of sight to the east. At this time we were thinking that this river was the one which came through the valley parallel and one north of ours although a little thought would have shown that it could not be. Thandu was of the opinion that it went to Nepal and was therefore of an entirely different 'jat'. Actually he was quite right as he realised that we were looking down into Tibet, while we with our minds on the small map had the idea that this was still a part of Sikkim.

A short calculation showed that we had no hope of safely attempting any alternative route home and so we resolved on a short trip down to the valley ahead of us to part satisfy our curiosity and a return whence we came. We set off down the most vile scree and took a dangerous route although I did not realise that until after CBS had started a slide and been caught up in it. I thought that he had broken his leg and had awful visions of trying to get him back to the camp and thence back to civilisation. Fortunately he emerged from it all as right as rain although a trifle shocked and we went on down in slightly worse order. CBS and the sirdar squatted down a few hundred feet above the glacier lake while I wandered about looking for photographs and generally seeing what the country was like. Except that there was no fuel and one would have to cross this pass to get here it is an excellent place for a base camp. The high mountains are only four thousand feet above the plateau and there are a whole string of them so that one could take one's choice and have a different problem every day. The rock work would be a bit rare but one cannot have all the joys at once.

Having chewed our ration of dates we retreated to the pass but this time took care to go beside a large snow bed where the scree was smaller, less steep and more stable. This route was safe enough and comfortable except in the very topmost stage where it was a bit thin but it was hard work all the way. We did not wait on the top but pressed on down leaving the sirdar to go on from the half way stage to prepare our tea for us. On one of the last alps we decided that it was so pleasant that there was no alternative but to sit down for the sheer joy of it. The evening was a perfect one although some of the clouds that were coming up were a bit menacing. Here we were embayed in a cirque of possible mountains – ones which one could walk around on — and could look out on to the cold snow of the higher places where greater skill was required. They were the

22 Thandu is the name of the sirdar.

target for the next visit to this country.

In camp CBS as Rationing Officer laid on the most magnificent of birthday feasts including a cake of the first water. I went to bed that night really content but knowing that the way from now on was homewards. Our plan was that if the morning was fine we would have another look up at the high mountains as I badly wanted to go and have a look at Chho Yummo from a bit closer. If however the weather was not so good we were to go down to Langpo and thence cross the The La down to Lachen in three days which is a generous allowance.

Saturday October 21st. The weather was not so good. There was a good deal of cloud about round the high summit which would have made sight seeing profitless while at our level there was a biting wind, once out of the shelter of our valley. So we headed south. The sahibs were some little way ahead of the rest, and going down the right of the Chakla Chu. When we came to the point, which I was not sure was the river we had originally meant to turn up for our pass over Rokcha, I could not resist going up to the first cirque to have a look around. It was twenty minutes up a yak track beside the pile of stones which does as a river till we came out into the cirque which was exciting in the extreme. In the sense that this was a more dramatic place than our valley it was a great pity that we did not come here in the first place but if we had done so we would probably have left it quickly by the easy route and not roamed up into the steep places. The pass we had had in mind was out of sight round to the left though we could see the first section which was steep and easy. More interesting was the view straight ahead where a glacier plunged down into the valley. I think one could get up either side of this which would lead one to a pleasant jumping off ground for a number of 19,000 ft and over peaks. It would be an interesting base camp too but this time there would be much more rock work to be done and the supply difficulties would be less. We only stayed a few minutes though I could have remained days but when we got back to the valley there was no sign of the coolies except for their foot prints. We turned right and pressed on. The path is of much of a muchness with the one on the opposite side of the valley and we saw nothing exciting except a pair of geese just above Mugotang. I had always heard that they migrated across the Himalayas but had never quite swallowed it. Here was proof.

What was not so good though was that here was also snow. A sudden shower of snow blew up from the south as we were coming into Mugotang and gave us a nasty fright. We had with us nothing of any use for the night and the porters were ahead and did not know where we were. It was thoroughly bad organisation again and I cursed myself heartily for it. At Mugotang itself there was a break in the cloud and I was able to see the last of the porters going over the horizon. When CBS come up I put on best speed hoping to cut off one of the porters from the rest. They were a long way off and as it was cold they were going like bombs. I gained on them but not sufficiently. Just as I was getting tired with the unaccustomed speed I came to the top of a hill and looked down to see some of the porters 200 yds away but on looking back I saw that CBS had become two so I presumed that I had over taken one of the porters by mistake. So I sat down and thought how wet and cold it would have been to spend the night in the open. When the two of them come up we continued down the path which is here a major track and let off steam on the subject of the sirdar allowing the party to get separated contrary to his express instructions. It is only the sahibs who can be allowed to get astray in this sort of country. Not long after we came to the site of Langpo where we found the party busy putting up tent. They explained that they had not been able to see the sahibs and thought that they had better camp. It was obvious that they had never thought of looking behind them and the real reason why they stopped was that it was a nasty day and they wanted some peace. The day should really have ended at another site called Langpo on the south side of the valley and near the foot of the The La. An even better place is just a little way up the route to the The La where there is a lake to provide water and plenty of fire wood.

However this time there was nothing much we could do about it, especially as we were to blame in not telling the men what our exact plans were. So we settled down to an unpleasant afternoon. We counted the stores and found that there was only just enough to take us back to Lachen. This again was bad but the rations were not calculated in advance in any detail as neither of us wanted to be dogmatic on a subject about which we knew absolutely nothing. About three it really began to come down hard and we evacuated the coolies tent to our own smaller one and nearly into our bags. There we had tea which made a large hole in some of the remaining stores. Soon after it showed some signs of clearing and I went out for the evening stroll. I went due west along the margin of the valley until I came to the Khora Chu where it comes down to the Lhonak from the north. From here I got a lovely view of the mountains at the head of this valley although they were blotched in cloud. It was down this valley that we would have come if our original plan had succeeded. This whole area between the Tibetan border and the Lhonak Chu fascinates me as here one can move around in the high places with only a modicum of difficulty and yet nobody does in fact so move. As far as I know these places are visited only by the yakherds and they do not much above the 17,000 ft, line. That night though, there was no time for speculation as the sun was even now setting behind the Langpo peaks and I had a long way to get back. I had a look at the bridge which we would have to cross in the morning as the main stream is a bit big for fording at this point. I then went down beside the stream until I was opposite the camp. In this way I was able to look back on the sunset behind the Langpo peaks which was first rate being a silhouette of two very fine mountains. With the sun gone the camp was a dreary place and I was quite glad to crawl into the bag and having eaten to drop off to sleep.

Sunday October 22nd. The morning was not too good as the lower valley was still choked with cloud as it had been all the previous afternoon. The wind over the The La which was just about due south of the camp was SE though over Kanchenjunga it was in the preferable SW. It looked to me as if it was the day to stay on the floor but the sirdar –rightly – said press on. On this stage only two of the coolies knew the route and that from a journey some three years before. We set off at round pace over the plain and were soon at the foot of the climb. There was said to be a path here but under the small layer of snow it was quite impossible to see it. As it was, the main lie of the route was obvious until we came over a shoulder into the main valley leading up to the pass. Being lazy they all traversed along at this point when it would have been much better to go down to the valley floor where the going was better. We floundered along over a snow covered scree and up and down steep banks which were difficult going for the coolies even with their present light loads.

After the first section of the valley it climbs and turns slightly right. At this stage we joined the path as it came up from below but immediately plunged into some soft snow drifts. The going was hard for the men but they made excellent progress. It was all I could do without any load other than the camera to keep up with them. Again it was the beneficial effect of the cold on their performance. The top was reached in less than the four hours we had allotted but the col was a miserable spot and the coolies went over it more or less at the double. When CBS had come up and one photograph had been taken we did the same and plunged down into a bank of fog. The hill was steep though not difficult. Somewhere on the way down we missed the track and got involved in a snow storm at the same time. There then began a long argument between the sirdar and the coolie who was supposed to know the way. The latter – truly – said that the path went along the side of the hill while the sirdar wanted to go down to the bottom. The sirdar was so timid that he had to be ordered to go down. This part was uncomfortable as it was over some bad scrub which was well covered in snow. In this valley it must have been snowing all the time as it was now deep on the floor. On the way up we had been able to see some of the peaks of the Upper Thonak and they appeared to be enjoying fine weather while south and west of it was snow. The Lhonak appears to be in the dry area of Tibet rather than in the monsoon area of the rest of Sikkim. This would mean that the glaciers are smaller and easier than the rest but we did not see many on which to test the theory.

Once we were down at the bottom of the hill it was obvious that there was no path along beside the Tomya Chu but it was in most places possible to walk along its snow covered banks. It was at this stage that my Itshide boots gave out completely. Whereas on other stuff I could stand where others could not, here on the mud covered stones beside the river I was quite helpless and sat down often. Luckily crawling alongside of a glacier stream does not have to be done frequently. We made progress along here very slowly for the best part of an hour until we came to a break in the grade where the stream took a plunge down into the depths below. We had to avoid this by a detour which the sirdar condescended to lead. At the top of the steep bank up which we were forced, we came on the path which was covered in snow but easy enough to see to the practiced eye. We had a rest at this point to consider further operations, as the sirdar, more out of jealousy as he did not know the route more than anything else, wanted to get down to Yatung a place which he knew, rather than stop at the Tomya Cave which was the coolies' idea. Actually it took us another hour to get to the cave and by that time it was nearly half past three and so we decided to stop there.

This cave consists of an overhanging rock which has had a wall built to close in the overhang and a small extension to the roof made of fir branches. It is set in a thick scrub somewhat below the rhododendron level and nearly at the tree line. It is the most draughty of places but the men preferred to sleep there rather than in their tent. Our tent was pitched a little way away in rather an uncomfortable spot but as we spent most of the time in the cave in an effort to get warm and dry again it did not matter much. Though my top held out well my trousers were not comfortable mainly because they had got soaked. I think that if one has any backing to a pair of windproof trousers it should be a very thin one indeed which will not press on the windproof surface. It was distinctly warmer this night which was not really surprising since we were down to 13,500 ft.

Monday October 23rd. The morning was not very fine and one could not see any exciting mountains though I do not think that there is anything very grand in this valley at the best of times. We were away rather late in the day what with one thing and another but the path was easy as it soon ran out of the snow and went down the valley in a gentlemanly manner. Opposite the end of the valley was the slope leading up to the Kishong La. This fascinated me at once as the path cuts a distinct zig-zag track on the hillside for all the 3,500 ft of its climb up from Yaktung to the top. I presumed therefore that the path is good at this stage though it is said that the rest of it down the Ta Lung Chu is the worst in the world or near it. I tried to find out how long it would take from here to Mangan by this direct route and the answer was four or five days. I should like to try this at the end of an expedition as I think that then one ought to be able to cut down on that time a bit although the coolies would be very peeved at not going back the normal easy way.

The last section of our path down to Yaktung fell through a forest of immense fir trees set in a bog of fir needles and other rotten vegetation. The top is not so bad but as one goes down the floor gets more and more water logged until one gets to the place where they lay logs in the mud, and one does a balancing act along the middle of them. When the rhododendrons come the fun becomes faster, as their leaves enrich the muddy compost and their roots provide at least half of the slippery foot holds. The coolies do magnificent work at these places as they hardly ever put a foot wrong. Their skill as porters seems to me to depend largely on their balance which is far better than mine can ever be.

Just before one reaches the bottom of the valley, the Green Lake path goes off to the right down a sniper slope to cross the Tomya Chu by a wooden bridge. Yakung itself is a wooden shanty with a small clearing round it, where travellers have cut the wood. As everywhere it is more of a marsh than anything else though beside the river, which is ten yards away, there is a dry moraine. We were in a most depressed place which had all the atmosphere of the last day of the holiday. It was low down – less than 12,000 ft – and in the depths of a forest of vast aged trees. The air heavy with damp and even the unaccustomed chirrup of the birds could not raise the gloom. We waited here for two of the porters to come up and then waded on down the valley.

The next section is probably the choice one as the marsh is deepest, and the most intriguing bits are vast lawns of bright green grass which look nice and inviting but in fact are greater swamps than all the rest put together. Across these the logs are laid in an irregular row and one is expected to tell by instinct under which part of the sea of mud they have sunk. If we had been carrying anything I am sure we would have stopped worrying and plunged in but as it was we jumped about all over the place in a vain effort to keep dry and clean. After a bit of this the path turns up through the forest which here looks more prehistoric than ever with the gauntness of the bare rhododendron branches added to the long drooping lichens hanging from the lower branches of the fir trees. We climbed for about four hundred feet and then turned right to do a sort of high level traverse through a number of yak alps. The yaks were apparently the dairy herd of Lachen and they had with them a lot of calves or whatever the young of yak are known as. We came across one man or woman – we were not able to decide on the sex with any certainty – who was greeted loudly by the porters and the whole party led off to their shanty which was on the next alp. This hut was a most drear place from the outside although the inside was tolerably comfortable. The pasture also was neglected and filled with weeds of one sort and another but the birds were there in simply glorious profusion. These fir woods must be among the best places in Sikkim for watching birds but I had no sufficient knowledge to even begin to look at them intelligently. Here the ravens were back on duty, the choughs having been left behind in sole charge of Lhonak. It is most curious how these two species were distributed, as above Dokyang they were all ravens, while in Lhomak they were all choughs. I wondered if it was anything to do with the lower rainfall in Lhonak which the choughs prefer.

This stop was ostensibly in aid of a cup of tea but it really was more in aid of a waste of time as it was only just after twelve and there was very little further to go. The tea with fresh yaks' milk was very good indeed but the rest of the entertainment was not so good as it was a cold depressing spot. Although there was no actual rain there was a good deal or cloud about in the higher regions and I think that it must have been snowing there. The last of the high mountains to be seen from near to is the ridge of the Zemu peak which can be seen from near Tsethang but even that seems a long way away and in a completely different world. In due course we came down to Tsethang which is a large and at that moment uninhabited alp just to the west of the point where the Lhonak Chu comes into the Zemu Chu. It was a remarkably pleasant spot distinguished by the dilapidated state of most of the huts. In view of the fact that the people have to live in them for a good deal of the time it is remarkable how little attention they give to any other than their town houses. They are nothing like as good as the typical Alpine chalet although the materials in the form of trees are just waiting to be cut down. But then in most countries you would not see so many fireplaces in the middle of the track where people have decided that they will spend the night. Along the main tracks there are many regular rocks where people lie up for the night and cook their cha and tsampa.

With no more than the usual delay we had some tea and the last of the flour was made into pancakes. These were our standby at this time of day and consisted of a dough of flour and water fried lightly in yak butter. Probably they were as hard as hell but in our state they slipped down at a rate of knots. After tea although it was not a very fine evening I went off for a walk hoping to be able to find the beginning of the path up the Lhonak Chu. I went out by the only entrance to the clearing that I could see and ended up on a one way track to the bridge across the Lhonak Chu. That did not seem very helpful as I knew that the path went up on the near side of the river and cast around the top edge of the clearing to find quite a fair path leading off in the right direction. This meandered along in a boggy way until it came to another clearing full of head high weeds. Here I lost the path again and had to cast around on the far side to find a path which was about half the size of the original one. In another few minutes the process was repeated and I began to think that this must be only a path leading to various clearings. But the second turned out to be the last of the clearings and a very narrow path led on up in a desultory sort of way just a little way above the stream. By all appearance it had not been used by more than one or two people since last spring and the weeds had grown all over it. A little way from its confluence within the Zemu Chu the Lhonak comes down a long straight race about half a mile long which though it provides a pleasant spectacle of white water has played hell with the path. Here there were many slips which had hardly been crossed at all since they had happened and on the other side of which there was often no sign of a path. I had been going for well over an hour and so I decided that here I would call it a day. I found a stream bed going uphill and went up some way to see if there was a view. I cannot really claim that there was although I took some pictures to commemorate the fact that I had spent so much effort getting such a short way. This track is definitely not to be included in a list of reasonable routes into and out of Lhonak. Seeing the state of the track I was surprised to hear that Murray and Marshall had come down this way. I imagine, despite their experience, that if there was no snow on the upper part one could do the thing in one long and hard day. But if there was no snow about every sensible man would be going over the The La so the interest in this route is largely academic. I trundled back to the camp in good time the way over the two clearings being very obvious when done in reverse.

In camp some more tea was on the brew and CBS had got a special fire laid on in the middle of nowhere where we could eat in real relative peace. By this time of course our appetites were admittedly large and a lot of the evening conversation was taken up in discussing the amount of food we would eat when we got to Lachen. This way of coming down to Lachen from Lhonak in three days is very idle indeed and leaves a mass of time for doing not very much which, as one is back in the close country, is not a good thing. We probably should have stayed at Yaktung and had a good half day from there and then moved down to Lachen in one go which would not have made a very great day. On this sort of stuff the advantage of knowing the route yourself is enormous as in all his statements the sirdar altered his times and distances to suit the argument of the moment. The best way of doing it to my mind is to camp a few hundred feet above the valley on the way up to the The La and then again at Yaktung, so making the journey in two good days. Done in this fashion this route is probably the best out of Lhonak though the Lungnak La is probably the best way in as there the daily climbs are not so great.

Tuesday October 24th. This was our last day off the bungalow routes and down at this level it was a fine one although up on the tops there was a bit of not so pleasant looking cloud. We started off across the Lhonak Chu crossing also a yak barrier on the path as the along on the far side of the river was occupied by cows and ne'er the two shall meet. From here on the path is not so wide as before nor so marshy but winds round and about near the river on quite dry stuff. The views of the river, which is by now quite a sizeable thing are very fine. It was one of the things which struck me up at Yaktung that the river was very small considering that it drained from one of the largest glaciers in the area. There were no excitements on this part except when we had to run through a cloud of some stinging bees which scored a hit apiece. This is not the sort of path I appreciate having to run along. At another place there had been a small slip for which there was no diversion for the coolies. One of the bright lads succeeded in falling over when being hauled up by the sirdar and flung his axe away in the process. This fortunately did not go far and was easily recovered. At the first major stream the coolies decided that washing was the order of the day although we thought it was still far too cold. Rather before eleven o'clock we came on to the main path from Lachen to Thangu. This was civilization, a wide path, a long suspension bridge, the smell of mule dung on the hot road – we had arrived. From here the path goes level along the right bank of the river while the latter goes farther and farther down into its gorge. In contrast to the sere grey of the pine forest and the brown of the upper regions this was a riot of autumn colours. In the forest there were occasional trees in the under growth which had a rich gold hue but here the whole hillside was ablaze with colour. I longed for a colour film as in black and white the scene was no better than prosaic. It is a short trundle into the village of Lachen which is first noticed by the prayer flags over a sort of tomb placed in the middle of the road just outside the village.

The village consists of about a hundred houses gathered together in a little east hollow with the monastery a little way up the hill behind. The dak bungalow is in the unusual position of being at the bottom of the village just below the road. The only other house of substance is the mansion of some Government official who we gathered had something to do with controlling the trade with Tibet. A new building was going up which I was told was the new school, the present school teacher being nearly ten miles away on the road to Thangu. It seems odd if that is so as most of the population of the valley must be centred in Lachen.

The houses of Lachen are very similar to those of Lachung although I think that they are even more uniform in design. Lachen is lucky in having some mortar in the region and upper parts of the houses are often made of a wattle and plaster mixture. This seems to need repair fairly often but lightens the load on the bottom part of the house. The method of building a bigger house is to expand the dimensions until one gets a large dark box. The idea of duplicating the structure in one house does not seem to have occurred to them. The women of the town were busy pounding away at barley from which I imagine they were to make tsampa. Barley and such things are grown in the town's fields which though they look scruffy and extreme must be fertile enough. The whole time we were in the higher part of Sikkim I do not remember having seen a soul working in the fields though compared to Switzerland they have far more arable land.

On arrival at the bungalow we had to get used to the idea of civilization. In one look in the mirror showed us how far away from it we had gone. The provision situation was not too bad and we were able to get hold of a shoulder and ribs of a goat or a sheep. One thing good to do in a journey up here is to buy a whole sheep and take it along as a week's meat ration. The trouble is that the supply is not very even as the beasts are grown in Tibet and only come down once in the year. A whole flock had passed through but two days before and the track was covered in their hoof marks.

Even sitting in chairs seemed a little strange and I was happier on the doorstep. The afternoon walk was not a great success as there is nowhere to go except along the track in one direction or the other. Unfortunately too the sun had gone in for its afternoon siesta and there was no light for the camera. That evening we did a sitting up late act and were in bed at eight only. Nevertheless we had only a short night before us as an early start had been decreed. The formal announcement that we were going to Toong in one had called a protest from the sirdar which was followed sharply by a storm from me. I am afraid that I found him rather soft on the subject of what a decent day's march was and got progressively shorter and shorter with him as I became fitter and he became nearer the end of the trek.

Wednesday October 25th. We did get off to an early start although I forgot to go and see the coolie of Murray's who had been left there. We had had a look at this man the day before and he seemed not too bad although he was sitting shivering in an open godown.[23] He and one other had come down by the The La one or two days ahead of us. We left at twenty to seven by our time, which was not right, and set off at a cracking pace. It was definitely back in shorts as the day before CBS had been complaining about the heat while he was coming down to Lachen. But for the first hour or two it was definitely also a pullover day. Just beyond the village the path plunged down into a deep gorge and then pulling up to the other side goes along through some delicious alpine meadows. This is one of the most pleasant of all the parts of the trek as it is open and non tropical while the mountains are all around even if they are not the highest. In this part there were many primulae particularly one with a long stalk with a deep blue cluster on the end. They began in the Zemu gorge and ended as the path swung down from this high level route. Like the birds I was very ignorant about the flowers of the country even though there were only about four species out at the time. The most impressive were the gentians although a little blue thing which I remembered well from the gardens at Cambridge was the delight of the slopes above the birthday camp.

Coming to the end of the alpine section the path plunges down through the forest to the river level. There it wanders along for a bit and crosses over. Here there were two bridges, one a suspension bridge at a high level which appeared to have a number of bits missing and lower a wooden bridge which I suppose was for animals. We decided that on this occasion we were animals and went down in to the depths. On the far bank were some people who were meant to be working on the road but promptly crowded round and demanded some baksheesh. We had really got back to the plains.

The path then wanders up and down the left bank of the river in quite good order until it gets down to the half way meadows. These are overgrown spots with a few old shacks scattered around where the herds retreat when it becomes tough going further up the valley. In the first place the path must gone down to Chungthang all the way like this but the flood has put a stop to that. Recently a gully on the right bank washed out and brought an immense amount of moraine down stream to block the river. Why this should have washed out and why the steam should have

---

23 Warehouse.

been running in moraine and not on rock is more than one can say. The mess is terrific and of course the great danger was that the dam would burst and flood the Tista. Indeed that was the first explanation of the September 14th disaster. In fact the river has carved away across the top of the dam and appears to be quite happy about it.

Which is more than can be said of the traveller. Instead of being able to go in comfort, along the bottom of the valley we had to climb about 1,300 ft up the side of the hill to get by. The side of the hill just opposite the washout is remarkably steep and the path could not have been cut round any lower. Even now looking up at it from the south it is hard to believe that the path goes where it does.

It was just as we had got on to the new bit of the path that we saw an apparition. As we were getting up a steep mudslope a full dressed Highlander appeared at the top and said hello or some such commonplace. He might have just have come out of the Edinburgh equivalent of Moss Bros., as except for a very highly polished Gurka Kukri[24] he was the perfect highland gentleman. But what a place to put on such an act. He was a tea planter and was heading for the Donkya La. I should have loved to have seen his kilt in the gales which blew us around that region. We were by this time looking exceeding disreputable with three weeks growth of beard and an almost equivalent growth of dirt on our clothes. The contrast must have been laughable especially as he was clean shaven – whether by art or nature we could not decide.

The powers that be evidently think that this diversion has come to stay as they are replacing the kutcha wood planking of the track by pukka stone embankments. They have not made much progress on the northern side but on the south work is nearly finished. We did not realise at the start how far we had to go up and it came as a shock to us when the path looked as though it was just going to turn one corner and drop down to Chungthang, when it turned on itself and zig-zagged further up. It did this for a long way and it took us just under an hour of hard and rapid work to reach the final summit from the foot of the diversion. The view from here was almost worth it. Across the other side of the valley was the tremendous gash which had caused all the trouble, while ahead – along way down – was Chungthang isolated on its peninsula. From here one can see the broad gash left by the flooding river and it is more remarkable that the bungalow survived.

It was just a romp down and we almost doubled some of the way. There is only one small break in the gradient all the way till just outside Chungthang. Down near the river on the right one can see some of the remains of the old road and a pleasant one it looks. The new one is still a bit raw and efficient with no subsequent slides to break the evenness and apparent high organisation of the whole. Just outside Chungthang there is one last slide which causes the dislocation of the routes which we had noticed before. Both the old main routes are no longer and one makes progress over the grass. On the meadow was the herd of sheep which we had been following down. There were about three hundred of them and they made a pretty sight.

We had lunch just the other side of the bridge; which was a silly place as we were in range of a party of Tibetan beggars. They really are the most unpleasant of people at times, always on the scrounge and quite phenomenally dirty. I think that there is nothing so annoying as beggars in the hills and they have no hope of getting anything out of me even as hush money. What they want more than anything is cigarettes and CBS's stub when thrown away caused a storm. As we were sitting and enjoying the sun the sheep were driven across the bridge and started on the next

24 Combat knife.

stage of their journey which they said was to Nanga, a village on the far side of Toong. They did not actually get there that night which was a very good thing as otherwise we would have had to pass them in the morning. As it was their moving was of no consequence as they were going by the diversion and we by the river route. We were not allowed to finish our rest in peace because of the Tibetan 'log'[25] and so we set off in not so good a mood to Toong. The river route had now become a major route and the path was in good order, though one or two more bits of the bank had come down and spread themselves over the path. By the time we had got back to a path again we were warmed up and ready for the fray. Actually this part of the fray is very good going and there are no difficulties until one comes to that slide which had given us such hard work on the way up. Here we got the shock of our lives as the thing had been transformed apparently by the group of men sitting and drinking tea at the bottom of it all. Instead of clambering up a creeper there was a vast platform built out of wood leading up the first bit and then a wide swath through the jungle down the far side. These chaps certainly know all about it when it comes to making a road fit for mules in double time.

A little farther on we met a crowd of sheep parked by the side of the road and I assume that it was to here only that the Chungthang lot came. There were two more slides between us and Toong bridge but we avoided both of them by using the river route which had been opened up since we had gone up. This went along beside the river over some comfortable moraine until it got round the corner just above the bridge. There it got a bit indefinite and we must have over shot the way up. Anyway, not so much further we got to a full stop where a rock dropped sheer to the river. We cast round and found a few marks in the mud of khud-side which might have been called a path. This led more or less vertically upward and deposited us sweating at every pore on the edge of the track just about at the place where we had lunch on the way up. We pressed on straight away and were soon down at the bridge again where everything had been tidied up, the only blot on the landscape being yet another party of Tibetans who promptly despatched their youngest child to whine after us. The bungalow at Toong is quite some way up the hill as is the tradition of bungalows. We arrived there two and a half hours from lunch which we considered fair going for the five miles of indifferent road.

It was yet early and there was no chance of the sirdar coming for at least an hour and a half so we tried to get something out of the chowkidar only to find that he was one of the dry rice merchants and could not even produce any fruit. The bungalow is a very small one and is of an earlier generation than the rest. It is used but seldom. In fact we were the first tourists to visit it that year. For all that it is a good place to break the journey on the way down. The two days of a stage and a half each are quite easy going even with the path in its present condition. I think that it would be possible to do it in two stages from Lachen to Gangtok as neither of these stages should take eleven hours each according to the times we put up. This part of the world is not very attractive and I think that it might as well be glossed over as rapidly as can be.

There is no possibility of taking an evening stroll here as there as there is only the road to stroll along and one will do that the next day if one has not already done it.

The sirdar turned up nearer to five than four which peeved us not a little and he did not display any great intelligence over the meal; the reason for this lapse did not strike us until the morrow. That night we pondered seriously on the question of a bath but decided against. It was

25 People.

still cold.

Thursday October 25th. To our surprise we were able to get away with another fairly early start this morning. And we needed it as we were going down into the deep valley where it would be hot. We had asked about the slip on this side of Dikchu which caused us such a lot of work on the way up and were told that it could be passed. So we thought that the whole day would he quite easy. The first seven miles are just work mildly against the engine of no particular interest to anybody. We set off round the back of the hut where there was an avoiding route to one of slips and which seemed to take us quite unnecessarily high up the mountain side. In three hours of not very fast going we passed the bungalow of Singhil and soon after came round the corner and looked down on the next section to Mangan. I was struck by the openness of the country. It seemed to have fallen back from the river in the three weeks that we had been away and much more of it seemed to have come under cultivation. In fact we had arrived at another stage of civilisation.

We had arrived too at another stage of heat, as the bazaar at Mangan was definitely warm. The place seems to be no better than a suntrap. It was full of sacks of cloves awaiting ponies to take them down to Gangtok, but far more to the point was the tea which was laid on in a very short time. When we were going up we had met here an old man who claimed to be on his way from Darjeeling to his 'Mullack' in Lachen. He was still there, looking very smart in a blue lined coat and his new but unlaced boots. He seemed to be the proprietor of the shop and I suppose what he meant to say that his family home was up in Lachen and he just came down here to make his money. Among other things he knew we were coming down and could tell us where we had been when we were up in the north.

When we had put down the tea we set off with the idea of having lunch at the Suspension Bridge. To our surprise both of us found that we were as stiff as can be. It was a very transient stiffness but even so if anybody had told me that one could suddenly stiffen as a result of a day's march after those weeks of hard effort in the mountains, I should not have believed him. I suppose that it was the sudden change from a short step to the long swinging pace we were using to get along these easy paths which did it. Whatever the cause the result was a serious limp for the first ten minutes after setting off.

On the way up we had found the bit up to the village very hard work but it was a romp down and we were soon on site for lunch on the other side of the bridge. By now it was nearing midday and getting hot though as yet we were not doing a powerful sweating act. The day before we had lasted out till the far side of Chungthang before drinking and this day until within two miles of Dikchu. From the bridge there is a stretch of easy country where the path had been damaged but had since been put right until we came to the liquor shop at Ralak. There we saw the path we had come down but took no notice of it. A little further on though, there was a block on the main road and an obvious diversion leading up to the left. This was evidently pukka as there was some work going on on it. We thought that this was some diversion round the worst of the slide. But the path went on and on up. In fact the going got steeper and we more and more bad tempered as it became obvious that we were going right back on to the path we had come by. It was slightly different as they had done a lot of work on it and it had improved by the passage of a large number of ponies. But it was still the same great height above the river. This climb in the heat had taken a lot out of me and I was glad to get down again. Nothing is more irritating than to be faced with this 800 ft climb at the end of the day when we had been led to believe that the path was in good order. For all we knew the lower damaged path was alright for humans while remaining unfit for mules. From the end of this entertainment it is only a short step into the bungalow at Dikchu. There the first of the paddy was being harvested although in some places on the hills above it been already finished. The chowkidar was slow in putting in an appearance but as we had remembered to bring some tea with us we were able to get that form of refreshment organised quickly. That and some oranges kept us quite happy until the sirdar deigned to put in an appearance at about five. This time we were in no doubt whatever that they were all as tight as lords. It does not seem to make them unsteady on their feet but just even more stupid than usual. In fact this night we could get no sense out of any of them. It was partly our fault for giving them an advance against their salary at Lachen but at that time I did not realise what it was going to be used for.

Again there is no place for the evening stroll at Dikchu and we spent the time reading, eating and drinking and this time we actually braved a bath. Down here in the depths there was no necessity to take elaborate precautions against the cold and so the bath was a success although there remained many layers of dirt to be removed. We calculated that we had had one bath in 17 days which sounds a bit grim but I defy anyone to like a bath up in the higher regions.

This evening we did another late bed act it being a little after eight when we clambered on to our beds, there being no question now of getting in to it. For all that we did not sleep that well as the atmosphere was an approximation to Calcutta. It had the same effect on our appetite which was temporarily reduced.

Friday October 27th. The last stage and as it turned out one of the easiest. We started out a bit late i.e. at ten to seven our time and set off at a round pace up the hill. We were not allowed to be in the shade for even half an hour and we were soon sweating hard. The path seemed transformed and a real high road, for instance in places the mules had two tracks instead of the one which is standard anywhere north; such was the change in our classification of roads. The path over the slip had been improved too and this was an objective and not merely a subjective change. It was not sufficiently good to ride a pony over it. It was amusing to note that we cut our time over the slip nearly by half, which only goes to show what habit does for one. The next bit we admitted to ourselves was a bit steep but as the sun had gone behind a cloud for some of the time it was not so unpleasant. We reached the top in just four hours and ten minutes which was rather faster than I had gone down hill three weeks before. We had lunch on the other side of the 'first, last and lowest' in a beautiful spot overlooking the valley of Gangtok.

From here it is a march along the highest of roads though one that seems to have little point in its existence, until at next to no time we were at the bungalow, having been greatly insulted by being tooted off the road by a car. On the way up I had found the milestones the most irritating reminders of the slow progress being made. But on the way back I hardly noticed any except on this last stretch down from the The La where every one was present. At this time I was in a fit state to time myself against and see that we exceeded the three mile an hour pace.

On arrival at the bungalow we indulged in an unseemly argument with the chowkidar who was insolent. This is the only occasion on which we vowed to take action in the bungalow book the next morning and actually got around to doing so. We put some cutting remarks in. The trouble was that he had to keep a room for a high official of the Central Government and merely told us that he was keeping the room for some other sahib; which attitude we did not like as the room offered us was worse than the accommodation offered in most of the higher bungalows. The man was not on good terms with the coolies either as he refused to lay on any wood and they had to go down to the bazaar. On the other hand he was doing the whole 'sab chiz' for our Bengali neighbour in the bungalow though I do not doubt that he was doing well on the cook's book.

When we were just preparing to stalk off in a rage the sirdar turned up having done a quick march from Dikchu and took over the tidying up of the affair. Meanwhile we set off for the bazaar where we visited the bank to recover that which we had deposited with them on the way up and then tried hard to scrounge some tea from them with complete lack of success. Instead we got hold of some sweets and biscuits and retired to the bungalow to gorge. This we did very satisfactorily.

Having eaten we encouraged the sirdar to get the barber and set off ourselves for the Post Office which is right at the top of the hill on which Gangtok is built. There we sent off two telegrams one to the Airways people and the other to DMG to lay on some food on our arrival on Saturday night. We had also found out from the bank that we could go on the mail bus to Tista Bridge if we were at a quarter to six in the morning when the bus would pick us up on its way down from the PO to the bazaar. We of course agreed to this and retired to have our faces shaved and hair cut with an easy conscience.

We were rather pleased with our performance on this day as we had come over from Dikchu in just the five hours and a half. This meant that our times for successive stages on the way down from Lachen were 5hrs 15min; 5hrs 30min; 5hrs 5min; and 5hrs 30min. That meant to us that one could come down in double stages without ruining oneself. It was only on the first stage down to Chungthang that we really flogged it and even then it was more for the joy of it than because we thought that we were short of time. The figures also mean that even the unfit could go up in three days to Lachen or Lachung instead of the normal four although whether this is desirable or not is quite another matter. It should be remembered in all these cases the routes traversed were a little damaged although I think that in most places these will remain the route for years to come.

The rest of the evening we just ate and got things organised, in between times admiring the mountains in the moon light. I was very annoyed that the mountains to be seen from Gangtok were never clear on either journey, not even clear enough to tempt one to take a photograph. On the way up from Dikchu to the pass we had been able to see some white mountain which was more than was possible on the way up country.

Saturday October 28th. We were up and about at an early hour and greatly to our surprise had everything organised in time when the bus arrived for us. We had a discussion with the chaps as to how much they should get for their services which was not so smooth as it might have been as I was determined that the sirdar should get no baksheesh in view of his scandalous behaviour up at Dokyang when we had such an uncomfortable night. He countered by saying that he had been asked to do coolies' work and all sorts of allegations to which we paid but scant attention.

Having finished with these matters and considering that the expedition was now over bar the shouting we piled into the front seat of honour and trundled down to the market. There we paraded up and down with the hooter blowing loudly until the owner-driver thought that he had an adequate load of passengers when we rolled off down the hill on the way home. It was quite a fine morning and although it was cool enough up in Gangtok when we were getting down into plains it became warm sitting as we were right on top of the engine.

The slip at the twelfth mile was now in perfect order while that at the nineteenth was only just passable. The back passengers had to get out while we crossed it and I am not so sure that if it had not been for questions of dignity at least two of the front passengers would not have done likewise. We next stopped in Rangpo while we spent quite some time while very little appeared to be done. At the Sikkim border we had to fill in the usual set of forms and sign ourselves out on the far side. We saw here that all the bullock carts came over the frontier bridge under man power and there appeared to be a number of men especially laid on for the job. Evasion of some law we presumed. What was definitely evasion of the loading laws was the fact that one passenger got off at Rangpo and walked across the border to be picked up on the other side of the frontier. The section from here on to the Tista Bridge was really in a bad way. Great chunks of the road had descended into the river or half way there and they were still working very hard trying to put it all to rights. Admittedly they had succeeded if the number of signs they had put up was a measure of success. Every bridge had a notice to go slow whereas they were the only parts of the road which were smooth enough to get up any pace on whatsoever.

On the far side of the Tista Bridge there was a conglomeration of trucks and cars one of which was to take the party down to the break at Giellekhola. This however was already full as to the front seat so we travelled second class. It took a long time to get all the goods from one lorry to the other and then a longer time still to get started. Once we had moved we had less than two miles to go before we got to the break. There were a lot of idle and feeble porters who demurred at taking our packs and had to be consoled with a special high rate. Needless to say at the other end they demanded extra for the hard work involved but equally needless to say they did not get it.

The break itself was quite a big one although the river must have gone very close to the road at the best of times. The powers that be had done nothing to repair it, while they had made an excellent diversion round the top complete with hand rail and steps. This was the scene of much activity as goods of all descriptions were going from lorries on one side to lorries on the other side. The other side is the railway station although the railway is completely closed and likely to remain so for some time as where the track has gone near to the river – which is most of the way – it has been completely wrecked. The next bus was not quite such a bright affair and it seemed to have a double load for the same capacity. This meant that we were uncomfortable for most of the way. The road winds through forests with the river at a varying distance down on the left and has been torn to bits in many places even this far down to the plains. Just near the King George bridge another car belonging to the same company had had a puncture so we all piled out while they rescued the one and only spare tyre from beneath our feet and a mountain of mail. From there it was not far to the plains which were most depressing. I had not realised that the Assam Rail Link bridge was so close to the hills. It is only a few hundred yards from the edge of the hills. We did not realise either that the Link was open again after its destruction by the floods. Apparently the reopening had been kept a bit quiet as they were doubtful it would carry the load and so did not want the Pakistani public to know too much about what went on. It was very obvious what an enormous amount of embankment had been washed away by the flood which 'band karoed'[26] the line.

From here to Siliguri is a matter of twelve dull miles and the driver was making us mad by coasting for a quarter of a mile and then accelerating for half and so on all way in to town. Siliguri gave the impression of great activity. There were countless new businesses being started, all I presume the result of Pakistan's having forced so much traffic through the town. Certainly the new station just to the north of the town is one of the finest buildings I have seen in India in the way of modern architecture.

When we got into town at the bus stop near the old station we found out that the arrangement made with the owner that we were to be dropped at the Airways (India) office had not penetrated

26 Stopped.

to the driver and in result we had come past it by about a mile. CBS laid on the charm and we were taken back to the place. There we were informed that there was no place on the plane, that our telegram had not arrived, that there would be no place until Tuesday, but if we liked we could go out to the aerodrome and take pot luck. I had been dreading that answer but it was one which could hardly have been avoided as we had no idea on the way up of how long it would take us to get back from Gangtok to the planes. Even though I was expecting it, it did not make it a lesser blow. We retired to the nearest eating house which was a Chinese restaurant just down the road and drowned our sorrows in an extremely hot curry. Even CBS admitted that it was warm. At this stage we were planning the action to be taken if one or none could get on the plane and had discovered that the Mail left at eleven o'clock and did not get into Sealdah until 7.30 the next morning, but one. That was a dim and grimy prospect. As can be imagined we were at the air company's office pretty sharp and waiting for that bus to take us out to the aerodrome, praying hard that a good number of people would miss it one way and another. Just a few minutes before we left another type turned up from Darjeeling on the same racket but he insisted on taking life very seriously and did not appear to relish the idea of a trip in the Link Express at all.

There were two freighters on the ground when we arrived and a mild and unsuccessful attempt was made to scrounge a lift on one of these. We then devoted our attention to hanging round the office desk to see that no one cut in on us and to watch the arrival of all those people who had remembered they had a plane to catch. We did not approve of them at all. The plane came in and disgorged a whole host of types who served to further confuse the situation. A quarter of an hour before we were due to leave they allowed us to exchange our vouchers for pukka tickets although nothing was definite as yet. Then we climbed into the plane and hoped that no one would rush up. But being last on the plane we had the bumpy seats near the tail. At long last came the shutting of the door and we were finally away on the last lap. Our companion at the back on this trip was a mad tea-planter who was coming down from the Dooars to get married. His wife was coming out on a plane from England later in the week and meanwhile he was going to have the hell of a time in Calcutta although he had not booked a room – which we thought a bit risky – nor for that matter had he got anything laid on about the marriage and we heard later that it had been a highly disorganised affair taken in hand at twelve hours notice by a friend of WB's [William Burridge].

It goes without saying that our appetites were by this time enormous and we polished off the plane's supply of food in no time at all. The journey was smooth enough and I had not a tinge of illness. We made a most efficient landing at Dum-Dum about twenty minutes ahead of schedule. There was the usual disorganisation while the luggage was given a fair wind and then we set off at a slow rate for Calcutta. The bus was of the most wheezey and we were nearly screaming mad by the time we manoeuvred into the place in Mission Row. There we took a taxi and the stray tea planter and took the one to the Grand which had rooms and to spare and the other to Bondel Road where DMG had given us up for lost and was on his way out to the pictures.

We sat down to a dinner of tinned meat.

And that was the end, the very end.

The expedition should really be regarded as a reconnaissance in force as the results from the mountaineering point of view were negligible – it being on two days only that we were off the beaten track. It must be admitted that these two days were quite the best of the lot, the enjoyment being not a little due to the fact that the map bore so little relation to the truth. But as a preview of the things to come the trip can be considered a success even from the technical angle. Its success as a holiday does not need to be mentioned – it was terrific. There were some problems of coolie pay and allowances which we were not quite clear about and which have since been checked up with those of great knowledge in these things. I am now in a position to state the complete terms of the bandobast and not rely on the honesty of the sirdar to state the right terms. This is quite an important point as they will always argue the toss and it is a great advantage to be sure of one's ground when refusing to meet their claims.

Not only have we some idea of what we expect the coolies to be able to do but also we have an idea of what we ourselves need to do and to carry about. The answer as far as clothes is warm and windproof and practically nothing else. We both took a great excess of clothes apparently thinking that standards of clothes in the plains of India would be continued in the hills. I was a bit apprehensive that the standards accepted in Europe would prove too uncomfortable in the Himalaya. In fact we found that the very minimum of changes was sufficient. After one had climbed out of the low valleys there are few occasion one gets really soaked with sweat. As has been said before for a very long time we lived in our clothes just taking on or off to suit the temperature and the activity. Though one needs but few changes one does need a lot of warm clothes as when it gets cold it takes no measures, and if one is cold there is no sleep and if there is no sleep there is an even grimmer than usual feeling in the morning.

We also discovered on the way back, when we were fit, we could do stages in a day and I can truthfully say that we enjoyed the extra half stage we did on the two days. It is one of the disadvantages of travel merely on the bungalow routes that one is so bound by the stages set by the PWD[27] one has hardly any choice left in deciding how far one will go in a day. Actually one is also bound by the porters whose capacity to carry is restricted by time or custom to a stage. This is a real disadvantage down in the lower parts as there it is next to impossible to get off the routes as there are so few paths and the country without paths is rather slow going. When one gets beyond the bungalows one is at one and the same time free of the restriction of the ground and of the PWD although one is still with the restriction of the porters who have very fixed places. It must be admitted that we did not take advantage of this freedom to do any long marches mainly because we were guided fairly closely by the interested advice of the sirdar to whom a long day was an anathema. We are therefore of the opinion that it is a very good thing to have one's own ideas of how long the day will be and announce to the world in general where the next camp will be. If one has not been to the part of the world before, it is of course a bit difficult to do this, but I think that it is worthwhile getting the information before and pretending one knows all about it. This of course may lead one into trouble or the Lhonak Chu.

We also can claim to know something about the technique of getting to Gangtok. I think that if the very early morning plane is running one has a hope of doing the journey in one day on the public transport. For one with an eye on costs it is obviously important to go on public transport if it is at all possible. Our journey down was a model of low cost traveling except in so far as we took the plane. It is however essential to take the plane as the train takes an age. If possible one should send the heavy luggage on Jetmull Bhojraj as that will save a lot of bother on the way and make one even better equipped for making use of the country transport system. The old cases of Allsopps lager were ideal for the job and should definitely be repeated. My own rucksack was not quite such

27 Public Works Department.

a success as I tried to take too much. A small pack for lunch when one is not on the move is a great asset.

Finance should be arranged with the state bank as it is not pleasant to take large sums around with you on the way up. This might cause a little difficulty in getting it out at the other end if one did the double stage from Singhik and arrived after the bank had closed and being highly organised left the following morning before it was open. Although it is a pleasant enough place to spend a bit of time, there is really no need to stay in Gangtok for any time at all as it is possible, if one knows what one wants, to get it all laid on previously. The trouble with this kind of efficiency is that then one would not have the excuse to go round and have a chat with all the officials in the town, which chat is a great consolation to them. It is almost a good turn for the day to go round and breathe a bit of life of the outside world into them.

And now we come to the most important result of the trip – do I want to go there again, and if so where to. The answer is of course that I am dying to go there again, and the second question is nearly as definitely answered. The country which really fascinated me was Lhonak where one can move around at relative ease at a great height, and where one is within range of all the biggest mountains in Sikkim. One can choose a mountain any desired height and if it is low enough one has a fair chance of getting up it. The difficulty with the area is that it is so far away from the world, Goma being three or four days beyond Thangu. However, in the process of getting there one gets fit to some extent and so the time is not entirely wasted. It is better to enter from Thangu, I think, from the point of view of acclimatisation. If one goes up the Zemu Chu one has the critical days on tracks while on the other route one is on the bungalow route for the first half of the danger zone. From Thangu there are two routes over the Lungnak La and the Metong and Tasha Las. As I have crossed the first named and not found anything too exciting, I think that the Metong La is indicated as the next move. I gather the Tasha La is used by the yak men while the Metong La is not known to have been crossed. From the west side it looks as though it ought not to be too difficult provided one remembers to take a turn to the north on crossing the col, thus avoiding a large ice-fall. From here I should like to go down the Chakla Chu for a mile or so and then turn up towards Rokcha and from a camp at about 16,000 ft spend a day or two reconnoitring the ridge between that cirque and the valley to the west. Having had a good look at that I should like to cross the ridge by whatever route appealed the most and then go back down to the Lhonak Chu a short way up the Lhonak and then turn south again to have a look at the area of the Hidden La and then the area a little nearer Tent Peak, with an attempt to get to Tent Peak Pass.

When time was drawing to a close a retreat could be made to the Zemu Glacier near the Green Lake and thence down the ordinary route to Yaktung. From here I would like to travel very light over the Kishong La down to Mangan. This is almost certainly a horrible route on most of the way but if one really went at it one should be able to do it in not more than the time taken to go round the normal way. From the point of view of camping in the leech world the trip should be taken when the brutes are not up to their tricks. And from Mangan one would of course do the double stage back to Gangtok and arrive absolutely flogged.

The problem remains to find the time, money, and companion. Firstly, a month, secondly, about Rs1,200 – this trip cost Rs900, all told, and thirdly a big question mark.

Calcutta, December 1950

Darjeeling

The jeep fills up

Lorry in difficulties

Tista at Tista Bridge

Mule

Near Gangtok

Gangtok

A glimpse of things ahead

Tista at Dikchu

A goat eats up the garden

Mangan

Paddy fields

Tista at Toong with man on the cane bridge

CBS crosses a small slide

Bridge at Lachung

Lamas at Lachung

Gorge cut by the flood

North from Yeumthang

Flood plain above Lachung

Dawn at Yeumthang

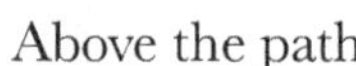

Above the path

The road to Mome Samdong

Grazing yak

On the way to the Sebu La

Tibetan yak at Mome Samdong

Tibetan yak at Mome Samdong

Chombu

Donkya Rhee

Glimpses of Pauhunri

Glimpses of Pauhunri

'Allsopps' rests beneath the Donkya La

Camp at 17,000'

Camp at 17,000'

On the way from Dokyang to Thangu

On the way from Dokyang to Thangu

From Thangu

Kanchenjunga & Tent Peak

Foot Tent Peak

3 views of Siniolchu from the Chakla Chu

Kanchenjunga & Tent Peak

To the East of the The La

Chho Yummo

A Tibetan Dzong beside the Chakla Chu

From the Chakla Chu

Chho Yummo

From Thandu La

From a little lower down

Peak to the South of the Metong La

Nearly-Tibet (Natu La)

Lachsi from Birthday Camp

From a spot just inside Tibet, to the NW

Due W

To the S

And where we came in, Thandu La

Looking forth to Tibet from below the Thandu La

Birthday Camp

A peak to the East of the Chakla Chu

To the South of Thandu La

A 1,900’ mountain with Thandu La (2,300’) on the right

View of a portion of Roka from Sikkim

View of a portion of Roka from Tibet

3 Scenes in the cirque below Rokcha where we should have gone

IN LHONAK
Looking up the Khora Chu

The Langpo Peaks at Sunset

Jonsong and Langpo Peaks

Dawn on the snow

The dammed-up lake in the Lachen Chu

Tomya Cave

A chalet in the Zemu Gorge

Last sight of a high hill

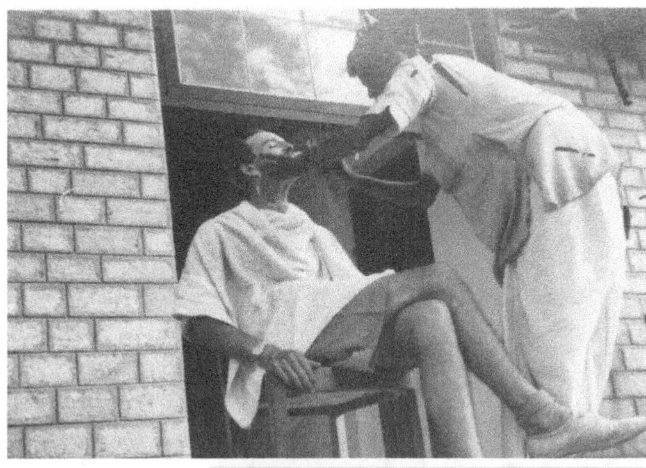

Us

And those who did the work

KULU AND LAHOUL

MAY – JUNE 1951

The file of correspondence on the subject of this trip was very much smaller than that for the trip to Sikkim, which was only partly due to the fact that the party was of one only; the main reason being that the trip had been planned in considerably less detail. Little information about the Kulu Valley was available in Calcutta and most of that news which I had came from Major Banon of Manali, and that was necessarily rather meagre.

Another deterrent to extensive organisation was the fact that the final plans had not been made till a week or so before D day as the firm had not been able to make up its mind as to whether I should be able to do some work for them in Delhi or no, upon which decision depended my day of entry into the hills. However, on the Saturday morning on which I left I was able to put most things in place and shortly before eleven I was to be found changing my shoes for boots in a taxi heading from Free School Street – where I had dumped my car for repairs – to the airway office. I believe in giving the airways a good weight to carry. It was inordinately hot – 107 in the shade – and wet as well. The airway office was very ill-ventilated and before five minutes were up I was wet through and feeling atrociously untidy. I had to pay the outrageous sum of Rs76 in excess freight and was duly warned by the collector that even so I might not be able to take it all on the plane. Fortunately for morale I did not take this statement very seriously.

We sweltered for a long time before the bus set off and crawled its weary way out to Dum Dum where there was another – considerable hiatus. I felt that I had just finished a two day journey rather than being at the beginning of it.

Somewhat behind schedule we were ushered on to the plane and there left to brew up a still greater heat. One might have expected some relief as soon as we started but it was not to be as the air vent opposite my seat was defunct; there was no other vacant seat. It was a most unpleasant journey which had best be forgotten about. Although the plane did not get flung around on a grand scale it was bumpy all the way and my inside was quite unable to compete.

Shortly after five we landed in Delhi. Going into the aerodrome building I got in the way of a fan and was scorched not cooled; we had arrived in the torrid zone. I left the bus at the Imperial and entered complete with my box of Allsopps to the general amusement of the hangers-on. The Reception Desk did not take very kindly to the idea of letting me have a room for such time as it would take to have a bath but were eventually persuaded. They gave me a very small room with three beds in it; but as luck would have it none of them were occupied. I called for a drink and set about preparing for the next leg of the journey.

Before I had got far in the process an American came in who had also come up on the plane from Calcutta. He was on a round-the-world trip with Pan Am who had slipped up and forgotten to reserve him a room for the night. He had only spent 48 hours in Calcutta but had seen more of the tourist sites in that time than I had in 20 months. He had some missionary connection and was duly shocked by Calcutta's depravities and not impressed nor even interested by its few accomplishments as a large centre of trade. He was now on his way to have a look at Agra and then to run back to the US as soon as he could. What a dismal way of travelling staying places just so long as to be able to say that one has been there. He was so deadly serious about all aspects of this world which we discussed that I am sure he must have been cut to the quick by the frivolous Calcutta approach, though may be staying only 48 hours he was preserved from having to listen to that.

I felt that I was more than a bit scruffy at dinner as my kit had been so pared as not to provide clean clothes for this evening. However I was in and out of the dining room before most people had ordered their pink gins and so no one was offended.

After dinner I took a taxi to the station, being agreeably surprised to find that it was only a five chip ride – I had memories of enormous taxi fares in January when they were on the firm. Delhi station was the usual shambles of an Indian railway station as the mail trains are about to leave. Cooks had managed to reserve me a place in a compartment which was only half full – the other half being a venerable and more or less harmless Sikh whose junior companions travelled in the second class compartment next door. I should add here that Cooks were only brought in because they could buy a cheap ticket for me for the Delhi – Pathankote run which could not be bought in Calcutta. For the rest they proved profoundly inefficient. There was about half an hour to wait during which time the Sikh gathered all his family into the compartment, and celebrated his departure. Fortunately though it was by no means hot and the platform was airy. A third character got into the carriage at the last moment but was only going to the first station down the line. The Sikh and he promptly started a long conversation on the outrageous cloth situation in the country and the various ways and means which could be employed to get round it. The effort of trying to translate the gabbled Hindí was too much and I soon fell asleep, before long diving beneath the blanket in an effort to keep warm – not that it was cold by most standards but railway trains seem to be degrees cooler than the surrounding country in the early hours of the morning. At first light we were passing through Jullundur and an Army officer and his small son both bound for Nagrota got on board, while the Sikh got off. I, however, tried to persuade myself that I was still able to sleep and did not show much sign of life until just before we ran into Amritsar at seven in the morning to find it a city which provides a face of uniformly blank walls to the traveller. One of the first things I had seen that morning was the River Beas which at this stage is wide and placid, much different from the swift gorgebound stream in which guise I was next to see it.

This was my first view of the Punjab countryside and I was duly impressed by the apparent great fertility and the fact that the people made an effort to get all they could out of the land. There were a large number of fields of some sort of clover which was being cut for fodder, while most of the other fields were stubble from the winters wheat crop, the winnowing of which was a common sight. The water wheels, a novel sight for me, were hard at work bringing up water for some of the crops which had just been sown.

Amritsar was the cue for breakfast and a tolerable meal was provided while the train dallied half an hour for us to eat it. The train reverses at this point and goes forward at a very leisurely pace making it hardly worthy of being called a mail train at all. It takes about two and three quarter hours to do the 67 miles into Pathankote.

At Amritsar we were joined by a rather grim half colonel of Gurkhas who was on his way up to rejoin his regiment in Kashmir. He was but one of a mass of military on the train, Pathankote itself looking more like Aldershot in the middle of the war than the gateway to the Himalayas. Such is the war in Kashmir.

One does not get more than an inkling of the proximity of the hills until one is nearly in Pathankote when at last one can see them looming up in a misty cloudiness all around. It was definitely getting hot when we arrived at 10.20 so the fan in the waiting room had taken the opportunity of going out of order while the washing facilities were quite non-existent.

The first thing to be done, paradoxically enough, was to arrange for a berth on the train back. As one is not meant to do this more than ten days before the date of the journey it needed a bit of persuasion though the man in charge seemed to be of more than average intelligence and in fact booked a good berth for me. Having fixed that I went for a stroll down the street. The station is some way from the old part of the town but with the enormous number of troops who are in the area, a whole bazaar has come into being, lining the road on both sides for the best part of a mile. It was all cheap and tawdry; the resemblance to the bastis[1] of Calcutta was lessened by the sight of two of the most dirty and unhappy looking camels strolling along with loads of wood. I do not think that I had ever seen camels out of zoos before; they were not impressive.

Before long I decided that there was nothing which I was tempted to do or see or buy and there being no other reason for remaining out in the hot sun I beat a retreat to the station where the fan had just come into action. The Kangra Valley train was due to leave at one o' clock and though the carriages were in the station long before then it did not seem likely that there would be much pressure on 1st class. We had rather less than three hours all told in Pathankote and when there was about an hour to go repaired to the Restaurant to be offered the most abominable of lunches. I could hardly eat a mouthful. My inside was in a bad way and I thought that I was in for an unpleasant time but the trouble cleared up rapidly; it must have been an after effect of the extreme disruption on the trip up from Calcutta to Delhi.

After lunch, my kit was taken to the train and we found that there were only two first class compartments; I had one to myself while the officer from Jullundur had the other. I laid in a few useful things like oranges and then went up to have a look at the engine. It was a pet. It chugged down on to the train about half an hour before we were due to leave and sat there looking rather helpless and doing its best to raise steam. The load was eight bogies but even so it had to work hard at some places to shift them up the grades. Just before we left the Janata Express came in from the south and disgorged a whole host on to the platform, fortunately few of whom seemed to be interested in our train. Two of the most jungly came up and tried in atrocious Hindi to ask some technical question about the running of our train. They did not get much sense out of me I am afraid.

Dead on time we chugged out stopping 220 yards later while they fixed the level crossing. It was something of an occasion if the train did more than thirty mph and more often the speed was about ten. However it was a persistent creature not stopping till the first station which is well over ten miles from Pathankote. The stations along the line were sprinkled with a lot of tough types wandering round with rifles over their shoulders There is a lot of jungle near here and I gather that the locals are keen shikaris,[2] the guns not being for the benefit of the Pakistanis.

It was very hot and I soon dozed off in the stuffy little carriage while the train toiled slowly up through the most barren of jungle and gorge country. It was dry, the rivers, such as they were, having hardly any water in their beds. Villages seemed to be just about non-existent. In time the train came to the half way station where it sat down to chew the cud and wait for the up train,

1 Shantytown.

2 Big game hunter or hunting guide.

which goes down, to come in. Meantime the guard wandered off to the local dukan[3] and enjoyed a smoke. This was my first introduction to the hubble bubble which is so attractive to the locals that they carry it in the fields as they shepherd their sheep. Smoking it is a most curious performance as, except at the beginning when the thing is getting going, the amount of smoke coming forth is small despite the great efforts of all concerned and some potent mixtures in the bowl beneath the charcoal – in the less well-equipped places a piece of smouldering string.

A little further up the valley there was a tea station and a Sikh dashed out with some tea together with the most cement like piece of cake which I have ever felt. My hunger was growing so I wolfed the lot and felt the better for it. After the dry jungle and barren gorges comes a more pastoral scene which could, with some imagination, be thought to be in Europe. The houses, sometimes two storeyed, are made of yellow washed mud, though the fact that it is mud is not obvious from a distance. Usually they are roofed with thatch though the richest ones have slates. They do not huddle together in compact villages but are grouped in twos and threes like English farmsteads.

From Pathankote one could see in the distance a line of mountains with their heads in the clouds and quite a bit of snow on them. The line wandered around up and down valleys but did not seem to make very much progress towards these mountains which one assumed were the goal. As a result I am not quite sure just how much the Kangra Valley is in fact a valley for it always appeared from the railway as though the easier way out was straight to the south, and indeed I did see a signpost near Kangra implying that one could get down to Jullundur that way. Be that as it may the railway follows a tortuous path which seems to be going up little more than it is going down though in fact it gains some two thousand feet in the course of the sixty odd miles to Nagrota. It is a fascinating railway, not for the great speeds it attains but for the casual way in which it tackles a one in forty slope or winds round hills, or doubles back on itself, or crosses nalas,[4] or just comes to a halt. Agreed it slows to a walking pace on the hills but the track wanders about without making any great attempt to keep to a level course.

About half past six we ran into Nagrota and were decanted from the train. It is a lonely sort of place with little sign of life apart from the station. The officer from Jullundur who was on his way up to a camp beyond Palampur had told me something about a bus which he was going to catch that night going on for the next 26 miles to Baijnath. I, however, had written making a reservation on that bus which was to leave at five the next morning, although whether that got all the way to Manali in one day was more than I could say. Luckily the porter who grabbed my luggage proved to be an intelligent fellow and he said that the Kulu bus left the next morning from the Himachal Government's Depot just down the road. So I trundled off there to find a place which looked like the remains of a dak bungalow with the verandah turned into a grain store. I was shown a room full of charpoys[5] where I could spend the night if I so wished. There was a chae-wallah's[6] shop just next door and he produced some tea and biscuits which quickly revived a fading form, fading more from lack of nourishment than excess of exercise.

However as soon as the transport clerks got to know that I was there they shoved me off to see

---

3 Shop.

4 Stream or gully.

5 Bed with frame and woven rope.

6 Tea person.

the station master apparently because they thought that the accommodation was not good enough for me and that I should stay instead in the station waiting room. However I thought that it would be simpler in the morning if I was where the bus started though I have no doubt that the bus would have picked me up from the station had I so wished.

By the time all the chatter was finished it was getting on for dark and so I went for a short walk down the road to the bazaar of Nagrota – not that there was anything of interest happening there. All the afternoon there had been a lot of thunder from the hills and we had had one or two light showers Now it was really setting about business and I had scarcely decided that it was about time that I returned when it began to drizzle. I stepped out and just made the bungalow before a most almighty thunder storm broke and drenched the place. By now the bungalow was alive with all sorts of people who were to spend the night there. Though they made a lot of noise I was quite weary enough to go to sleep straight away and not hungry enough to be kept awake by the pangs. The night was warm for all our 2,800 ft and there was no question at all of getting in to the sleeping bag.

The next morning, not long after four, there was a noise outside as the bus started up and roared off down to the Post Office to fetch the mail. Someone identified the noise for me and so I got up and packed my things – that is to say I rolled up the bed-roll in which most things were already stuffed. I had only two pieces of luggage – the bed-roll and the beer crate – as the two tents and the ice axes were rolled into the middle of the bed. Outside it was hardly showing the first sign of dawn, more light coming from countless glow worms than from the sun. As the light came up one could see that the hills still had cloud around the snow level though not as much as the night before.

I spent an eternity wandering up and down waiting for the bus to come back from the village. When it did there was a further delay while I paid all of Rs14-6-0 being the fare to Manali. As the journey was to take 14 hours I thought that this was good value for money. Even so it was a bit before five when the bus had collected itself together and set off. This was the mail bus and so had to stop at all the hamlets giving forth loud toots on the horn to try and get from his bed the local post man and give him the mail. This at five in the morning required hard work. Before many minutes were up and before even fewer miles had been passed we came to Palampur where we parked for further doings with the mail. Palampur is a pleasant sort of place which used to be the centre of a number of tea gardens which were largely damaged by an earthquake in 1905 passing thereafter into Indian hands in which they do not appear to have prospered. It is now of course more famous as a regimental centre of the Gurkhas.

The bus belonged to the Himachal Pradesh Government. It appears that not so long ago a company which used to have a half share in the Kulu Valley traffic went bust and the Government took over the services they used to operate. They have done very well indeed as the service they now have is most efficient and all their staff are polite and helpful. Judging by the number of forms which they fill in the previous company must have died of corruption. It would be difficult indeed to cheat this concern – all their vehicles are Dodge chassis with either a passenger body or a covered van built on to it. The passenger accommodation consists of five upper class seats and a larger number of lower. However the larger number seems to be defined as they often refused to take any more aboard. Indeed it seemed to be necessary to be a personal friend of the driver to get picked up at any but the major stops. The rival firm in the business is the Kulu Valley Transport Company whose equipment is antique in the extreme and in addition they do not believe in answering letters or any such modern technique. I was lucky to travel nationalised.

In the end, we moved off from Palampur and trundled down the hill to Baijnath which is a dirty place of some religious significance. We did not wait there long but pressed on up to Jogindernagar famous for an enormous power station. We arrived at about half past seven and here at last there was a stop for refreshment; a large cup of steaming hot and sweet tea was soon poured down.

The road so far had been an excellent one and though in some places it would not have been possible to pass, that hardly mattered at this hour of the morning. However from Jogindernagar to Mandi there is a system of one way traffic in operation and one does a ten mile stretch only to come up against a chain across the road, everyone queues up and in time a policeman is persuaded to come forth and unlock a padlock and let down the chain. Then the whole mass of buses and trucks tear off to the other end of the stretch where they again queue up and await the undoing of another padlock.

Between Baijnath and Jogindernagar one enters Himachal Pradesh where all the policemen controlling the road are gay in their blue and yellow turbans as opposed to the more drab red and blue of the Punjab. Though the road goes through Himachal Pradesh it is maintained by the Punjab Government at Central expense except for a short section in Mandi itself.

Just beyond Jogindernagar the road goes over the top at about five thousand feet. So far one has been more or less hugging the feet of the mountains that lie to the north and getting along to the west as best one can. Over the pass one drops down by a circuitous route to the gorge of the Beas. In this part of the State there are a large number of salt mines run by the Government of India. They seem to evaporate down the water which runs off from the salt bearing rocks.

About ten in the morning we ran into Mandi. This is an unpleasant place, though except for the number of flies, there seems to be no apparent reason for it being so. It nestles beside the Beas which is crossed here by an antique Suspension Bridge built in the 1870s with appropriate Gothic decoration. There is a man to walk in front of the car bearing a board stating that he is doing this to force one to drive at the prescribed speed of four miles an hour. From the temple-lined river the one and only road in the town climbs up to the main square which is oblong and houses the bazaar and then slips past the Law Courts to arrive in a sort of Parliament Square in the centre of which is a sunken garden which was a mass of Jacaranda blossom.

It was hot and the aggressive Hinduism of the town, which though it is in the hills, is filled with people who stroll around in the sloppy hand-holding manner of the Desi log[7] rather jarred. The buildings are most charming – especially the main offices of the Government which have a delicious high swinging gabled roof with wooden shingles – and even the wood-built two-storeyed bazaar had a certain attraction while a house in the course of erection down by the river contained some choice carved woodwork. I went round some of the back ways while the bus was changing the mail, finding that though the buildings were in themselves pleasant the whole effect was odious.

We were due to leave within the hour but what with one thing and another we were over three quarters of an hour late getting away. The driver was a bit harassed trying to pacify those who wanted to get on but for whom there was no room and at the same time getting some refreshment for himself. The flies put me off the refreshment despite the fact that I was as hungry as could be, my stomach having quite recovered from the day before's indisposition. I had only a cup of tea and

7 Indigenous people.

that out in the open air on the balustrade of the sunken garden making thereby a great sight for the idlers of the town – and they seemed to constitute the majority of the population.

We set off again with tempers a bit frayed by the heat and dust. The road crossed a small side stream by a rather more substantial bridge than that over the Beas and then runs past the junk heap of the Company which the Government has taken over – which heap is appropriately enough nearly opposite the depot of the new concern. The road then becomes one way again but less notice is taken on this part and one is liable to meet someone going the other way; except at Aut there are no police to control the traffic.

From here on the road is unmetalled and spectacular in the extreme. It suffices to say that it caught my breath equally on the way up as on the way down. The first twelve miles to Pandoh are tame enough except in so far as there is no stretch of the road straight for more than 50 yards at a time. One goes along the valley of the Beas on its west bank through more or less deserted country all the houses being further up the hillside. Gentle hills rising several thousand feet on either side are covered in jungle to their tops.

At Pandoh there is another of the four mile an hour bridges and thereafter one enters the Aut gorges where the gods obviously did not intend the road to go. For the next ten miles it crawls around the cliffs, sometimes cut out of the rock and always within inches of sudden death, the cliffs often being sheer for thousands of feet. There is no life in this section except for some small slate workings. Lower down in the Kangra Valley we had passed some flocks of sheep on their way up to the summer pastures but fortunately we met none on this section of road as otherwise there would have been some casualties. The sheep on their way up to Manali take a short cut across the hills and miss out Mandi altogether.

As it was we flung some goods off the top of the bus but they hit the one bit of the verge from which they would not fall into the river below. My kit being about the first on was in a firm position and I did not feel more than usually anxious about its safety.

About a mile from Aut we were stopped by the roving ticket collector who actually did inspect the tickets and was profuse in his apologies to me for causing the delay – nationalised transport is efficient hereabouts. At this point the road to Simla is on the opposite side of the valley – it is said to be jeepable all the way but reports state that it is wiser to walk about sixty miles out of the one hundred and four. If this road was only made pucca[8] it would greatly ease the problem of getting to the Kulu Valley and should make the place even more prosperous than it is at present.

Aut is a dingy little place of not more than a dozen houses most of which seem to exist to sell refreshment to those awaiting the dropping of the chain to go through on the next road section. From here on to Manali the road is also one way but as there are no police on the job no one takes any notice at all and the hazards are added to not inconsiderably.

About three miles above Aut the gorge widens to form the Kulu Valley proper. The afternoon was cloudy and sultry and I was most unimpressed by it all. It looked just like any other part of India – dry, parched earth banks between the empty fields – altogether rather miserable. Its prosperity seems to lie in the fact that one can get two crops to the year with ease and its fame on the facility with which one can grow all sorts of temperate plants. Higher up the valley there are a whole host of plant breeding and research stations taking advantage of this.

We were still only conscious of the heat and not the health. We were decanted at Kulu and

---

8 Good.

told that there was an hour and a half to wait before we went on. It looked like rain. I was tired and hungry. The bazaar was even filthier than the one in Mandi and I could not bring myself to like the idea of even a cup of tea here.

Kulu is built in two pieces. There is a sort of upper town where the offices and dak bungalow are, all of which are strewn around the fringes of an attractive maidan;[9] and there is the lower town where we were parked which is one long bazaar of inordinate filth. There was only one thing to do – walk up it until I got out into the fresh air. I was too weary to go far so I sat down by the river and took in the scene – and actually enjoyed a wash in the cold water. I remember saying at the time that that would be the last time I would want to wash in cold water for a very long while –it was.

I was just on my way back to the bus when the threatened storm burst and so taking shelter in a shop's verandah I watched the road become a river. This was in all ways a monotonous bazaar as the buildings were identical; the living quarters on the first floor and the workroom or shop on the second with a small covered verandah facing the street.

The rain was quickly over and I went back to the bus office to find that the bus had gone off to fetch the mail. There was nothing to do but sit around and get cold as the wind whistled round my bare knees. By the time the bus turned up it had started raining again and we set off on the last lap of 23 miles in a downpour.

As a result of all the rain the main street of the bazaar was a river through which we charged blowing the horn loudly and watching the inhabitants jumping for dear life. Beyond the town the road had been turned into a morasse and as it frequently goes along incuts in moraine cliffs it felt most unsafe. I thought that we were definitely out of control on one occasion when we started slipping in the mud half way up a steep slide with the river twenty feet below. However what could one do? The road always seemed to be banked up on the inward side – had a bias towards the Beas in fact.

Midway between Kulu and Manali the character of the valley changes and from a version of the plains of India it becomes a version of the Alps. And what a version. The whole thing is on a larger scale and hills which look so small as not to be worthy of notice will in fact take you more than a day to climb. Manali itself is set up on the side of the valley at the foot of a steep wooded slope looking out over the fields which are at this time of year the brilliant green of growing barley. Lower down by Kulu the crop was being harvested but up here at a height of a little more than six thousand feet would be another two months or more before the fields were cleared. The bus stopped at a place called Duff Dunbar which is in effect the Manali of common parlance although the village proper is a mile further on up an even rougher road. Here is the dak bungalow and the Post Office and a small bazaar. More important is the fact that the road to Lahoul here crosses the river and sets off on its 46 mile journey to Keylang as a large notice board announces to the world.

Up to Kulu the mileposts are from Amritsar – and from there on from Kulu. They extend for about a hundred miles from Kulu to some place just beyond the last bungalow at Patseo on the way to the Baralacha La.

Major Banon had arranged for someone in the way of a sirdar to await me and a chap jumped forth as soon as I got out of the bus, proudly displaying his brass badge which announced that he was a registered shikari. The kit tumbled off the top of the bus and was set in motion for Major Banon's place which is about half a mile up the road to Manali. With all the talk of

9 Square, open space.

the amazing orchards of Manali in particular and of Kulu in general I had expected to see acres and acres of first rate trees and was rather disappointed by the actual thing. The trees are rather misshapen and seem to be strewn about the place in a haphazard manner – not that there were a lot of them even then. Before my arrival, I had not realised that there were two brothers by the name of Banon both of whom run orchards but only one of whom runs a hotel as well. This rather foxed me as a little before Manali a European boarded the bus who obviously lived in the valley and he was said to be Major Banon. However as soon as I started talking to him he mentioned pointedly that it was his brother who deals with the tourist angle. He devotes his time to hanging round the Post Office to all appearance though his orchards are as large as his brothers.

All the way up from Nagrota I had been looked upon by the locals as a very curious being and so I had the impression that Europeans were now a rare phenomenon in the valley. I was soon put right when I found that Banon had a full house of them, so full that he had a tent in the garden for me. On arrival I had some most welcome tea and thereafter an even more welcome bath in a tin tub in the tent.

When that was done it was time to go up to the house and set about the meal. The rest of the party hailed from Delhi and belonged mainly to the world of officialdom and learning, except for an American consular couple who were up for only two days or so and seemed to be at sea in such company. Certainly I was, as in the town of Calcutta, I never come across people who are not in one way or another involved in the making of money, an occupation which I sensed these did not quite approve of. I felt even more uncomfortable because together with the early start of the morning I had not done a shave and I was determined to let the beard grow to provide some small protection against the elements.

Pines are the feature of this part – tall upstanding trees standing in a carpet of their own needles and not so close together as to impede progress. Beside the stream coming down from the Manali Nala were a couple of water mills. These work with a horizontal water wheel on which impinges a jet of water created by a twelve foot channel leading down from the mill. The water wheel is below the mill store which, in the ones which I saw, is of the upper stone moving. The grain is automatically fed from a basket suspended above the stones and so no attention is required. Indeed they often lock the door of the mill and leave it to run all day. Otherwise they depute a boy or girl to sit over it and go to sleep. These little square boxes and the water leats leading up to them are a very common feature both in Kulu and Lahoul and they are all of identical design, though down in the Kangra Valley I did see one of a very advanced type in which there was a vertical water wheel geared to the vertical shaft as are the irrigation wheels of the Punjab.

Crossing this stream I climbed up a short bank and looked back to the mountains to the east of the valley; this morning there was not much cloud about and one could see the full extent of the snow fields which came well down into the valleys. The peaks which one could see were of the order of eighteen thousand feet but as the last eight of these were in snow they looked more impressive than their height warranted. There were one or two which had most spectacular rock pinnacles perched on relatively broad snowy shoulders. These should provide a lot of sport at the end of the year.

I was back at the tent at seven and found some tea waiting for me which went down well as I began to get the kit organised for movement. The arrangement was that the sirdar would turn up at eight in the morning and we would then make the bandobast. This he did and we arranged that the coolies should arrive at two in the afternoon prepared for a three weeks' journey in Lahoul. The hotel clerk aided and abetted in all this and one way and another I was forced to accept six coolies as the minimum as they were only capable of humping 40 pounds. This was a blow as all my calculations had been based on the Sikkim standard of 60 pounds per man. This was but the first occasion on which my previous experience was found to be irrelevant at this, about the other, end of the Himalayas. With the aid of the hotel people I got hold of the remaining few items of food which I wanted; though in the process we forgot salt which would have been a disaster had it not been for the coolies' supplies.

Salt is a very important commodity up here. The pastures are deficient in it and on their way up from the lower valleys the sheep carry with them – together with their shepherds' food – a certain amount of salt for themselves. If one is stranded without the stuff oneself one might as well give up as it is an absolutely essential ingredient of all the masses one eats.

Having got the basic principles of transport fixed I had breakfast, and afterwards tried to collect all information possible from Peck. He was very informative though he had not been over to the far side of the Rohtang. He suggested that on arrival in the Chamba Valley I turn right and march for some way, instead of merely going up and down the nearest suitable mountain as I had had in mind. I should then try to return to Kulu over a pass known as the Sare Umga pass which crosses the range to the south of Putti Runni, a camping place on the Khoksar-Spiti track some 23 days trek from Khoksar. This sounded fun to me as the pass is not now used by the locals and its crossing would take me through some country which looked lovely on the map.

I was very keen on getting into Lahoul for many reasons though I realised that it might be a bit early in the year; perhaps the most weighty factor was that I have an incurable itch to see around the corner. If one stays in Kulu one is likely to make only two-three day expeditions from base at Manali which would mean remaining a bit close to civilisation for liking. Another reason perhaps was that I even then realised that Lahoul was approaching the Tibetan zone and I prefer that to the areas south of the Great Himalaya which have affinities to India rather than to the dry lands to the north. It might have been possible to go over to the Chamba Valley by the Hampta Pass which is a thousand feet higher than the Rohtang and is much less used, and lands one one day nearer Putti Runni; but I thought that it would be better to let the clutch in gently. It was as well that I did.

Having more or less decided what was to be done I went down to the village to see if I could arrange a seat on the bus on the way back. It seems a depressing thing to do at the beginning of a holiday but it was essential that the arrangements for getting back to Delhi were as infallible as they could be made. However the office of the Government Transport was closed as it was the day for the mid-day service to be run by their rival and the aforesaid rivals did not seem to be functioning either, although there was a decrepit bus waiting to go down to Kulu. In the end I gave up waiting for the clerk who was always said to be just coming and returning to the hotel asked the clerk there if he could fix it. The bus companies could do with a joint booking service as the complication of having alternate services run by each company makes it impossible for even the locals to know off hand which concern is doing the work on any given day.

The rest of the morning was spent loafing around hoping that the clouds would not return and wondering whether any coolies would turn up at the appointed hour. They did; but they were not a very keen looking bunch. They were wearing the felted jodhpurs which are the common dress round here and long heavy shirts of a similar material which I gather is made by them in their villages usually from the wool of their own sheep. On their heads they have little round caps with a three quarter brim turned up to lie flush with the skull. The pouch formed thereby makes a very useful receptacle for flowers gathered by the way side; the blooms show to their best in them.

With them these coolies had the communal hubble bubble and various lengths of rope. They do not carry the stuff in the same way as the Sherpas, the whole weight being taken by ropes passing over the shoulders after the manner of rucksacks. Whether this is the reason or not they are not half such good porters as the Sherpas; indeed they hardly qualify for the name porters at all. The ropes over the shoulder are a constant source of trouble as they are fixed by a sort of slip knot which seems capable of slipping the wrong way when anything goes wrong. They like to take with them a big stick with which to hoist themselves from the ground after one of their many rests. They make out that it is a great effort standing up with forty pounds on one's back but I fail to remember that the Sherpas made anything like such a fuss about lifting a load half as much again. It took a goodly time to sort the things out and for everybody to be convinced that they were not being hardly done by in the matter of loads.

At about three however we were all set for the road and while the coolies went off by themselves the sirdar and I went down to the village to get some last minute things including cigarettes for the boys. I bought some 750 of these for a lot less than ten chips and hoped that it was a good investment. They really prefer their pipe which comes out and is passed around at almost every halt but they smoke cigarettes if free. The sirdar establishes his supremacy in this vital matter by taking with him a private supply. They used to burn the most peculiar things in their pipe varying from something which might possibly have been tobacco to wood chips.

The road crosses the river just behind the dak bungalow and then turns up beside the river which it follows fairly closely. About a mile from the start there is a little shop where one can buy last minute thoughts and here we found all the coolies lying about doing nothing. Something was wrong though I was unable to find out quite what. After giving them time for a smoke I moved them on but went ahead myself with the sirdar. This meant that the coolies did absolutely nothing and half an hour later were about 25 minutes behind.

The first stage, up to the bungalow at Kothi, is about seven miles and two thousand feet. It is easy going all the way. For the first five miles or so one follows the left bank of the river with particularly good views of the mountains round the Solang Nala to the North West. The mountains directly behind Manali are quite impressive from here though they are of no great height and are distinguished more by their rocky abruptness. Manalik Nala itself is a sizable affair and from its head a pass crosses over to the next valley to the West which would be fun to try although it is said to be closed at this time of year and judging by the snow to be seen I can well believe it. There is also a path marked over from the head of the Solang but this does not seem to be known to the locals. Perhaps the reason is that on the other side it goes down over a glacier and they seem to have the greatest distaste for travelling over snow. They think that if there is snow in any place it follows that no one can want to go there whereas I feel that the reverse is more true if one lives in the plains for the rest of the year.

About two miles from the bungalow the path crosses the Beas by a temporary bridge – the old one being reconstructed after the winter damage. The path then wanders round circuitously to avoid a 500 ft escarpment. The fields here are among the highest in the valley to carry barley and they were barely in ear though they were the most vivid green I can ever remember seeing – a colour which was shortly to be surpassed in Lahoul. At the top of the escarpment the sirdar called us to a halt allegedly for the coolies but really because he wanted a smoke himself. At last we saw them far below straggling along by the river and so we pushed on for the final mile up to the bungalow.

Some way back we had come across the bungalow jemedar[10] on the way down to Manali for some leave and he was only persuaded to turn about and come back to work with difficulty. It really seemed to worry him and the chowkidar that I had not a permit to occupy the place, and we spent quite some time cursing them before they opened the bungalow. In the morning I was shown a notice which quite clearly said that the bungalow was not to be opened without a permit except in cases of emergency, and the chowkidar here really believed it. In Lahoul they had a rather more healthy attitude to such regulations and did not seem concerned about the absence of a pass at all. The bungalow stands a little way above the track which had at this point climbed up from the river and is about to contour along the hill to the disused bungalow at Rahla. The Kothi bungalow is a luxurious affair compared to the rest, but was short of crockery. One thing which should be remembered is that these bungalows do not have curtains to use as emergency blankets although they do have carpets; but these look as though they would be uncomfortable in the extreme.

Round the bungalow are a number of fields which were at this time ploughed although the numerous flocks of sheep were spending a lot of time wandering about over the plough apparently with the intention of fertilising the fields as they were often left there for the night. The height of the bungalow is about 8,500 ft and as it was six when we arrived it soon started to get cold though the coolies were yet afar off. My heart sank and I thought that I had really got hold of a dud lot if they could not do better than this on a mere seven mile stage – or was it just that it was the first day and they were getting into their stride? Eventually, when I was just considering the easiest way of getting the carpet up and using it as a rug the coolies came in sight far down the hillside. I was glad of that cup of tea which their arrival made possible. Thereafter, I determined to wear long trousers or keep with the Crew.

Rashly I had said that I would eat corned beef that night and in due course a horrid hash was produced which was forced down somehow. But when I got to bed I could not sleep and at length at midnight or so I realised that I was going to be sick. I did not approve of the corned beef. It was not an auspicious beginning to the trip.

As a result on the next morning I was not over full of bounce and was not running around first thing stimulating the chaps into action. Indeed by the time I had had breakfast it was obvious that we were not going to get over the pass by mid-day as all the pundits say one should, in order to avoid the wind. I am not sure whether or not it was a good thing to miss this one day but at the time I remember thinking that it would be as well to get some training done as it might happen that I would be really altitude sick on the top at thirteen thousand coming up as quickly as I had done from the plains. Anyway it was decided that I should go off on a reconnaissance to see what conditions were like as no one seemed to be quite sure even now whether it was possible to cross the pass. Or maybe it was that they were not sure if I could do it and that was their way of putting it.

Another potent reason for putting off departure for a day was that negotiations for a sheep were incomplete. The price was to be thirty chips which was an awful lot to pay for the skinny thing but I was determined to have some meat in Lahoul and I did not think that there was much chance of getting it there as proved to be the case. The coolies also were very keen on the idea. I thought at first that they would say that they could not take it over to Lahoul alive but it was not so – snow is no obstacle to one sheep though it may be to hundreds.

So I set off up the road for the pass. The first two miles is up the valley to the old bungalow

10 Official.

at Rahla. This is a pleasant stretch through open pine woods with steeper forests raising on each side. The river is crossed just below the bungalow which is now a shambles. At the time it was inhabited by a lot of Spitiotis whose few belongings were scattered about the living room and whose animals were grazing around the outhouses. This is the highest house in the valley at about 8,800 ft although the highest farm is down at Kothi. Just beyond the bungalow the path goes into a steep climb and gets up 1,200 ft in less than no time. Later I discovered that there is an even more direct route which goes up a sort of staircase of slabs but even the bridle track itself is a real thigh basher.

The view to the south expands rapidly whilst before one the mountains take on more specific form. They were smothered in snow which came down to the top of the steep section at about ten thousand. The route thereafter levels out but the track trodden in the snow took an independent course as the locals, being impatient, had not bothered to follow the zigzags of the road. Judging by the footprints in the snow a number of people had gone to and fro over the pass since the last fall so I presumed that there was no great difficulty in the passage.

After crossing this more or less level place the path takes to the left slope of the valley and edges its way along. Down to the right is a narrow gorge which at this time was filled with avalanche debris and looked most unpleasant. Beyond that the mountains rose to about eighteen thousand in long snow slopes with rock outcrops at the top. The trouble with most of the slopes from the climbing point of view was that they were obviously swept by avalanches though I think that one could engineer a devious route up most of the peaks which one can see from this path at even this time of year.

At about twelve thousand the path comes to an impressive nala which is the traveller's tale of these parts. The south wall is very steep indeed though the north is merely a long snow slope. The track wanders along a ledge on the south wall and then crosses – rapidly I am glad to say – a small avalanche shoot at the head of the gully. This ledge is not wide and at this time half filled with wet snow. The PWD men had been making an attempt to cut a track but they had only half completed the work and in so doing had made life more difficult rather than easier.

Once over this – in which there is no real difficulty – the route is a smooth climb up to the summit. Whatever it may look like from far away this is in fact another thigh basher as it is continuous hard work up a deceptively gentle looking slope. The snow was not in too bad condition and where it had been trodden one did not sink in, though off the path one went in ankle deep at the least. The snow was covered with a thaw crust which went tinkling off into the depths at every step but which did not have any tendency to avalanche. The pass is a wide open space between two thousand foot slopes leading up to unimpressive mountains. The actual col is rather to the left of centre and there is not much of a view from it as to the north is a long gentle snow slope for a mile or so until the ground drops away with a whoosh to the valley while to the right a small rise blocks the view.

But the mountains on the far side.

There was virtually no rock to be seen except where the ground was so steep that snow would not lie, and the slopes of this dazzling snow were up to eight thousand feet long. All the hills were much of a muchness as to size and rather alike in form with steep shoulders leading up to high swinging ridges with few cols on them. The way up to the mountains seemed to be up the nalas to the glaciers from some places on which large snow beds led up to the tops. However the entrances to the nalas were very narrow and steep and by the look of the thing by no means too safe whereas once inside the nalas widened substantially.

From the strict top of the pass I went a few hundred feet right to get a better view of the valley and to take some photographs. I had been told that one should be off the pass by mid-day as thereafter a great wind got up which makes life uncomfortable if not dangerous. It was not so, as though in the early morning there had been a gale blowing down at the bungalow, at mid-day on the top it was possible to stand around for twenty minutes taking it all in and not get more than damn cold. Of course I was well covered up for the trip but even so it was by no means frigid nor was there anything in the way of a wind though I admit that had there been one it would have been a truly uninviting spot.

Having looked around to my heart's content I set off back finding the PWD coolies hard at work at the nala cutting the snow out and shovelling it down hill to oblivion. They cannot have done more than four hours work in a day as they came up all the way from Kothi. Why the PWD do not build a shack above Rahla and make them live there I cannot think. Just below the nala I thought it was time for a rest and found a convenient rock on which to perch and let some of the day go by. In the early morning the wind was from the north which slackening gave way to the south wind by mid-day or so. This latter brought with it a lot of cloud which gathered around some of the tops looking a bit ominous. It usually happened that the cloud blew away again in the night and the morning would break fine.

Lying on my rock I wondered how lucky I had been not to have felt any effects of the height. The top is 13,050 ft and though I had not been there for long I had come up from the plains at a good rate and should not have been exceptionally fit. This first day was about fourteen miles and 4,500 ft each way – which is not a small start. But I never felt any stiffness or undue tiredness – and this though I had not had all that much exercise in town just prior to this leave. I cannot think why this should be but it suggest that a lot of this training stuff is so much nonsense.

Awaking from my reverie I went down the hill at none too great a speed being not a little put off by the steepness of the descent to Rahla. The last two miles is a delightful way of finishing off the day as there is nothing to do in the way of work and a lot to do in the way of looking at the world.

I arrived back in a conscious glow of self-satisfaction on seeing all the coolies hanging around doing absolutely nothing. They gave appropriately great salaams to acknowledge their day of rest. I was glad to see that meantime we had acquired a sheep and I was even more glad to get a cup of tea inside. Intentionally I had brought nothing with me from the world below in the way of books so in the evening I had nothing to do but chew a pipe and gaze around the place, the bungalows being devoid of any literature with but one exception.

Here at Kothi I learnt a lot which would have been more appropriately learnt in the divinity class at school. It is a reflection either on the teachers or on the pupil that I had not really taken these things in before. The sheep and goats go round in large flocks herded by the boys and young men of the villages. They roam all day on the steep slopes and at night go to some sheltered place such as under a rock or on the village fields and while the shepherds light a fire the sheep settle themselves to sleep. No nonsense about dogs to keep them in order – they seem to realise that they are there for the night and that there is nothing to be done about it. Shepherds watch their flocks by night in fact. Also the difficulty of telling the sheep from the goats is evident as they go round as one and though of a slightly different shape are not easily distinguished. The simplest way of separating them would be to hold a race over a steep place when the goats will forge ahead. And David obviously learnt his skill with the sling flinging stones to keep the flocks going in the right direction.

The animals have an incredible sense of the flock and if a stone lands near them they promptly start for the main body which is not necessarily the same thing as away from the stone. The only thing that I did remember from my school days was that the shepherd went in front of his flock but here at any rate they have the military police at the rear encouraging all and sundry to keep up. Oddly enough there are dogs attached to these flocks but they seem to be there for decoration only.

I slept soundly that night having done my best to drive home to the chaps the point that I wanted to get away early. They obviously did not really think that in the morning it was necessary to do so as though tea arrived at about half five it was nearer half seven before the caravan started off. At this stage of proceedings I was not good at bouncing around trying to get action at an early hour of the morning and preferred to let them take their own time. It was not as it had been in Sikkim that we wanted to get off in the cool of the morning to make full use of daylight of which there is enough at this time of year for one to be a little extravagant. It got light about five and dark at about half seven.

Even straight after the start and with the light loads that they had progress was slow in the extreme and so my apprehensions in respect of the coolies grew. They were not equipped in the usual sense of the word. Some of them had shoes but they did not like wearing them, preferring their polas – rice straw sandals. The combination of shoes and socks was quite unheard of. None of them had dark glasses although the PWD coolies were all so equipped. Their clothing was not too bad but hardly designed for sitting down in wet snow which they so frequently did.

The first major halt was taken by the Rahla bungalow where loads were dumped and the pipe started up. Once the thing has got going it seems rather a pity to stop it and they always take ages getting it packed up for action. That is one advantage of a cigarette – it takes a definite time to be finished and then there is no excuse for not going on.

Straight away from the halt they went up the short cut which was larger than the one I was fool enough to take for the first day or two in Sikkim. But I thought that as I was paying them I could confine my activity to cursing them in my most fluent Hindustani. Towards the top of the steep portion my patience wore thin and I forged ahead over the level stretch to a bare spot just where the path begins to contour along the hillside. This was quite fatal as when I was behind them they did make some progress, but if I was in front they gave up hope and let me go right out into the blue while they sat down and did nothing.

I had been sitting on my chosen perch for some time before they even came in sight and then they had the nerve to sit down again about a couple of hundred feet below me. They sat there so long that I became quite worked up about it all and sent the sirdar down to fix them – not that he did.

The sheep was doing magnificent work, though in the lower and greener places she showed a tendency to wander off, only to be hauled back on the string; once up in the snow where there was not much alternative, she followed along peacefully, sometimes even leading the party. After the chaps had so misbehaved themselves I stayed back and led my army from the rear. This is undoubtedly the right way to deal with them, though exasperating. I tried to vary the monotony by getting pictures of them as though they were hard at work in the most spectacularly steep and or desolate places. It was a slow process as they were more often cooling their bottoms in the snow. It took us just six hours and a quarter to climb the 4,500 ft from the bungalow to the summit. As the top was not a very inviting place we went down the gentle slope to the edge of an escarpment where the path disappeared over a rock face. There was a bare bit of rock on which we sat. Even the coolies then expressed some interest in the valley before them – especially one who had not seen it before. They agreed that they had not seen so much snow in the place for a long time though I suspected that this might have been for my benefit as they knew that I wanted to go up the valley. Just opposite to this point is the Kulti Nala which is surrounded by some of the best of the mountains in Lahoul forming a nearly uncrossable chain. To the right somewhere above Putti Runni there were a couple of outstanding giants which offered no lines of weakness while to the left above Khoksar there was a magnificent line of cliffs buttressing a mountain which was possibly the most photogenic of the lot. And nowhere could one see any trace of man except for the tracks at ones feet; though this in a couple of months time was to be one of the busiest passes in the country.

Actually a little way to the left of our resting place there was a hut which is used as a rest place but we did not see it as it was so smothered in snow. The path from here on went down a really fierce snow slope which, being in the shade, was frozen and made distinctly unpleasant going for the chaps with their loads. For me of course it was an absolute gift as I could glissade down the hard bits and stamp down the soft. I gave up leading the army from behind for a bit of frolic until I came to a convenient rock which was still in the sun and there I sat and waited for them. The map marks the escarpment crossing as almost half way along the route to Khoksar (which is considerably to the west of the pass), but I thought that I had gone as far again and yet there was no sign of the place.

What had happened was that the path had fallen off the top too soon. After a seeming age the chaps came up looking tired by it all, as well they might as they had been at work for a long time. Unusually enough they had had some chuppattis to eat at half time. These are not a bad thing in the middle of the day though I, of course, stuck rigidly to my biscuits and raisins.

When we started off on the final lap I went ahead again as I did not think it likely that they would delay long with the end in sight, and romped down to the bungalow. The road was under snow nearly all the way but was good going as it was well graded and the snow was crisp. The bungalow is on the south bank of the river connected by a spindly looking bridge to the hamlet of Damphu. This consists of two houses looking out from a scarp over the river and a gompa[11] in the cliffs at the back. The highest cultivation in the valley is at the hamlet of North Khoksar which is about a mile up the valley from Damphu. The whole scene was mottled with snow and in the cold light of a cloudy evening was most harsh. I thought that Khoksar was a miserable place and said so to the sirdar who remarked that all Lahoul was like this place.

I was more depressed by the accumulating evidence that it was not going to be possible to go up the river. I had set my heart on going to the west as it was away from habitations and nobody seemed to know much about it. It soon was obvious why, as there was no wood to be seen near the bungalow although the coolies arranged some for their fire while mine cost a fantastic price bought from the chowkidar. Although on the map one can see that half a day up stream there is a forest of hazel or some such and in fact can see the sparse trees from the track these are no good for fires until they have been dried. The stuff which is wanted is the same as the Sherpas used in Sikkim and is here known as dubh. But whereas it grows up to 16,000 ft in Lahoul, here it hardly gets to eleven. That evening I had a long discussion with the sirdar to try and find out what the situation was and if there was any way at all of going up, but he was adamant that the road would not be open for a month or two and at the moment it was nothing other than dangerous to go up there;

11 Buddhist fortification.

in fact, he said, the coolies would die. There was not even enough wood in Khoksar to enable us to take a couple of days supply and go for a rapid survey. I thought of going up the mountains using Khoksar as a base but apart from the fact that they looked difficult in the extreme they would not last one the whole time and so might well be time wasted. I came to the conclusion later that I will never make a Himalayan climber as I am far too anxious to see round the corner. In these mountains there are always such a host of corners to see round, which not many have examined before, that I always find myself pressing on.

The Khoksar bungalow is a minute place consisting of two rooms with their porches and bathrooms and an intercommunicating door between. The rooms are about as long as a charpoy and scarcely wider. The outside was whitewashed and capped with the usual red tin roof but the plaster was all falling away and the tin roof looked blotchy. In addition a lot of the glass had blown out of the windows even though they were protected with wire netting.

As compensation for all this damage the place sported two mirrors so I was able to examine the state of my face. It was bad. The snow had done its worst on the first day, though at the time I had been quite happy about it.

In the morning I paid a call on the PWD babu[12] who was based on the hut and asked him about the state of the roads. He unfortunately supported the sirdar in every word, in so far as I could understand him as all the conversation was in Hindi. So reluctantly I had to give the orders for going down the valley. But at the same time I got rid of one of the coolies. I tried to get rid of two but they maintained that five were essential and as I did not want to have to give a practical demonstration I let it go at that.

Keylang is three stages away from Khoksar but only 27 miles and there are no obstacles on the way. I thought therefore that we ought to be able to reach the capital of Lahoul in two easy days. As usual there was opposition from all concerned, but the babu had to agree that one could do the first two stages to Gondla in a day, as it was only 16 or 17 miles. That, however, was first thing in the morning when I was ready to go. By the time the extra man had been paid off and the chaps persuaded that we were going down that day, it was declared too late to do the two stages and not knowing the country I was hardly in a position to deny it.

It was a grey morning which later cheered up to a brilliant sunny day to welcome us at Sissu, the first bungalow about eight miles from Khoksar. The valley at Khoksar is very steep and narrow and at this time was largely packed with snow which had formed great bridges over the river. One crosses the river just below the bungalow and for all the rest of the way the path is more or less near the right bank of the river. After a narrow section culminating in a cliff crawl the valley opens out to allow the smallest of fields which were quite empty and deserted. Sissu itself lies way above the river on a little plateau overlooking the vast desert of scree which was beside the river, then partly submerged in snow waters.

At about the first stop we met the dak walla going the other way. He was an active old man and only stopped to light a cigarette before forcing on at a cracking pace. When taxed with their idleness compared to this ancient, the chaps said that it was all due to their heavy loads – the liars! As may be guessed I did not bear with them all day but pressed on ahead when they stopped for the third time in a quarter of a mile. The path was easy enough as all the snow was well packed after the winter and did not let one sink at all.

---

12 Government official.

At one place I remember noticing that on the surface of the snow there were a lot of bits of fir twig while there was not a tree in sight on the slope above. It was only after on the way back that I found that these bits of twig came from a sparse copse way up on the other side of the valley and had been carried across the river by the avalanches. This must be a wicked place in the winter.

After the valley widens out habitations begin, though to start with they are all on the shelf on the north side of the valley above the path.

We got to Sissu rather after two, having made a bad passage more through frustration at not being able to go where I had intended, than anything else.

The bungalow at Sissu is among the most charming spots I have ever seen. As I have said it is on a ledge above the river and the scarp down to the river is clothed in a willow plantation. Trees do not grow wild in this country and so they get such wood as they can from a sort of willow. These are planted in rows or in fields and irrigation ducts are led around their roots. Every seven years or so they are pollarded to a height of about ten feet and the proceeds form excellent fire wood. In a place where sheep and goats are often hungry and wander around without restraint one might think the end of trees would be barked and that would be it; but the Lahoulis have one good enough for that. The trees are propagated by cutting down ten year branches, lopping both ends and sticking one in the ground. As an anti gnaw move one plants four or five in a tight clump so that no animal can possibly twist its nose in such a way as to gnaw the centre bark. So the trees survive, though in the more civilised parts they wrap them up in thorn as an extra precaution for the first year or two.

When we arrived at Sissu the buds were just breaking and so for the first time for two years I could see what spring should look like. It was a thrill – one had forgotten in the lush tropical fecundity of Bengal what it was to see a tree or shrub or plant or even a blade of grass which was starting to grow just because it had at last become warm enough to make it worthwhile. Maybe the green which resulted was an ordinary green – possibly even the green of Ireland would make it look drab, but the fact remains that the sight of the budding trees of Sissu and the few acres of grass behind houses appeared to me streets ahead of the first sight of the emerald isle from the sea.

One could indeed feel that the world was coming back to life and with that sensation one felt that an extra degree of perception was coming to oneself.

More logically I think that the virtue of the colour scheme lay in the contrast of the vegetable green to the mineral greys and browns of the rocks together with the purest blue of sky and the whitest white of snow. Put together it was enough to make one delirious.

Instead of going mad, though, I got the sirdar to produce some tea which I drank sitting out on the maidan outside the bungalow lapping up the miracle which was around me. The bungalow itself, though of the standard design of two rooms and a red roof, came to look like a charming country cottage set in its well kept lawns.

Sissu village proper is further on the way to Keylang, there being on their side of the nala only the dak bungalow and three or four houses. The Lahoulis build a house wherever there is ground to plough, though if there is enough land to support two families or more, the houses are all built close together

As it never rains in Lahoul – a lie containing the basis of a truth – the houses do not have to cope with water – to the casual glance they do not look capable of doing so. They are flatroofed blank sided boxes built of stone with wooden joists, the whole being plastered over with a grey plaster. Decorations are rare and if they are present, are usually on the wood work rather than on the plaster. Though these houses are almost the antithesis of an Alpine chalet the smell of a Lahouli village might have been imported from the Valais and ripened on the way. In the Alps the central feature of the village is often the washing stone, but in Lahoul it is quite absent and I feel sure that it would not be used even if some kind soul inserted one.

After my tea I shot up the hill behind and quickly got entangled in a thorn covered khud-side in which paths of soft snow alternated with slippery mud. I could see some way ahead a line contouring round the hillside and thought that this would be a good way up the Sissu Nala, so I headed for it. On arrival I found that it was the remains of an irrigation channel which was in a very bad state of repair. I followed it out to the end of a spur where the channel had completely disappeared and found myself on a slope of gravel lying at an appalling angle with no visible means of support. The only route was up – so I went up. All was well for some way though it did occur to me that it might be difficult to get down again, but on the ridge the going really did begin to get 'mushkil'.[13] It necessitated getting the ice axe to work on cutting steps in the gravel. A week later I would have taken it as read, but at this stage I had not learnt at what a fantastic angle gravel can lie and yet remain safe in this country of no rain.

Luckily I arrived at the top with only a scratch and found a slope leading up to the ridge bounding the nala to the west, which was irresistible. I went up a tongue of bare earth for some way and then transferred to the snow for the last pull up. As luck would have it this snow was in excellent condition and except near rock outcrops one could rattle along as fast as the muscles and breath would allow. At the chosen site on the ridge I stopped for a look around. The Sissu Nala extends for a long way up into the heart of the mountains but could hardly be said to be a route unless one can go up just beside the stream, which I doubt. On the east side there is a magnificent and quite impossible line of cliff and scree while on my side there was a deal of this gravel stuff which while passable for one, would hardly do as a route for the coolies, while higher up there were unbroken snow slopes. A trip like this brings home sharply how difficult it may be to travel in these mountains once one gets off the beaten. To take a party up this nala would involve going well up in the snow on the west slope and even then I would hesitate to prophesy an even passage. All around were mountains in grade one, though all much of a muchness in that grade. I was standing on a shoulder of – and therefore could not see – the Gephorn, which is maybe the most famous in Lahoul, but certainly the most spectacular were the mountains on the other side of the Chamba.

Shikar Beh is a bit over 20,000 ft and drops in one long slope of rock and ice to the Chamba at under 10,000 ft. I would defy anyone to even plan a route up this face so steep and icy is it. One would not even be able to make a start. The Rohtang and the Hampta Passes seem to be lucky exceptions, in a strongly defended wall, consisting of the Shikar Beh group and those ferocious things to be seen frowning down in the valley to the east of Khoksar.

After taking a round of photographs I rushed down the slope to the fields at the bottom, this time following all the snow slopes that I could as they made life so much easier. Back at camp the coolies had arrived and were sitting round a fire thinking about boiling their share – the lion's – of the sheep whose slaughter had been decreed. The night before there had not been enough wood to make a good fire to roast the thing by. My share of the animal at this stage was its liver and kidneys. You have no idea how much of these accessories even a small sheep can carry about with it. When I had eaten supper and so bloated out was I that I could hardly move from the table – I was convinced that I had eaten the lot and was greatly disconcerted to find the following morning

13 Difficult or struggle.

that I only had had half to my credit.

In the evening I wandered round the village and had a look at what was going on. The answer was remarkably little, other than the planting of some potatoes in a tiny field by the road. The road at this point was more or less taken up by a prayer wall though no one seemed to take much notice of it. I was told that this wall was for the lama log only; though every village worthy of the name would point out with pride its gompas tucked away in the cliffs. These people are Buddhists rather nominally and may be said to live in a state of not being Hindu.

In the morning we were not away at a very early hour as there seemed remarkably little point in being so when there were only nine miles to go. The coolies were quite firm that one could not do the stage from Sissu to Keylang in one, although I would take on to do the whole thing, Keylang to Khoksar, in one if need be. After a very few miles I ran off my map as I had not bought any of this area, not that I could have anyway, as they are restricted. Thereafter it was real exploration to me although it was on a broad highway. There is a lot to be said for not having a map with you as it adds a fresh spice in rounding every corner.

I really got 'hopping mad' with the chaps this morning when after ten minutes work they all sat down for a rest. Telling them what I thought of them in my best Hindustani, liberally pattered with the easier adjectives of my own language, I pressed on at full speed – to Gondla, and in so doing I left the sirdar well behind; he also having decided that this 'sahib' was a bit much of a good thing. This is rather a pastoral day as one is going through inhabited places all the way though most of the houses are well above the road where the ground shelves slightly. On the way we stopped to watch the beginning of the ploughing season by a family. About ten adults were engaged and half as many children. They came along, one leading the yaks, one carrying the plough, another the yoke, a fourth the hubble-bubble and the most important the god, a wooden skittle with a bulbous top. The plough was not quite the same as in the plains of India as the share, instead of being a mere point, was a flat heartshaped piece of iron which was pushed along about two inches below the surface. The yaks were hitched to the plough and the whole manoeuvred into position while the god was sitting on his platter. When all was ready the god was brought to the plough, the yaks, and the ploughmen. Then a vast wail burst forth and the yaks moved off led by one man while another followed vainly trying to keep the plough on an even keel. The soil is friable enough and it ploughs more easily than most of the stuff in the plains.

Just before Gondla one passes a large house built on the same lines as all the rest but on a larger scale. This is the house of the Thakur Sahib who seems to be the aristocrat of the district and whose houses are regularly pointed out. Just above the village is another house of fame. It is the skyscraper of Lahoul and to add to the dizzy effect it is perched on a rock above the road. I was told that the idea had been to build it yet another storey high but they discovered that they had not built straight and so had to give up. Even as it is the top storey looks as though it was an after thought as it is surrounded by a verandah built out from the stone walls on flimsy wooden joists.

The bungalow is right beneath the road and below overlooks the fields of the village and the river. Being lower down the valley things were more advanced than in Sissu, but somehow they had lost that element of surprise – perhaps because there was not such a sharply drawn contrast between the green of the fields and the barren hillside; although opposite the village on the south bank of the river there rose quite the fiercest of cliffs nearly smothered in snow which frequently burst into rumbling avalanches. Just below the bungalow a family was engaged in enlarging a field by building up the lynchet with stone walling and filling with earth the gap between the new wall and the old part. It was the girls who did all the horrid work of moving earth while the men occasionally turned to and shifted an enormous stone by a foot or two. As I was coming down the last few feet to the bungalow I heard two sharp explosions and thought that perhaps the Pakistanis had made a large raid since I left the newspapers behind. But it was not that – it was just these types blowing up a couple of boulders which were in the middle of their new field. Progress in remotest Lahoul.

The chowkidar was a long lanky cadaverous type who at the time I thought was very helpful but on the way back I came to the conclusion that he was an utter rogue as, having failed to sell the sirdar eggs at 4as. each, he came along and tried the sahib, thinking that I would not know what he had been doing with the sirdar. He was most disappointed that I did not leap at the offer as he probably knew we had not been able to get any eggs at all in any other village in the valley.

As may be imagined I was very anxious to rid myself of the coolies and I was hopeful as for the last miles in from Sissu there had been a lot of ponies on the road, though none of them had been seen at work. Enquiries were set on foot and it appeared that one of the types who was so diligently sitting on his bottom in the field below might be able to help. He was called up and negotiations commenced on the step of the verandah – I worried the chowkidar a lot by not sitting in the chair he had brought out for me. It seemed that I might be able to get the services of a pony for Rs5 a stage and half that on a day off. As my present caravan was costing Rs15 day in day out this was obviously a good thing, though I believe that the correct rate later in the year when there is a lot of traffic moving is Rs3 only. There was some discussion as to whether one pony could take the whole load, but this was pure 'chalaki'[14] as in fact it was easy work for him.

Having, I thought, settled the business I climbed off up the hill behind the village. There is from here a path over to Keylang on which General Bruce got lost, but I was told that at this time of year the descent down to Keylang was unsafe and on looking at it from that side I can well believe it to be so. On this side though, the slope is one of the gentlest in the district, but largely covered in snow. I climbed up for the best part of two hours to a point where three pillars gave an excuse for stopping and some respite from the wind. The view was one of the best that I had had, mainly because one was then standing back from the mountains which otherwise tend to be foreshortented by their steepness. Opposite the mighty slopes of Shikar Beh rose in one unbroken face while a little to their right a magnificent broken glacier led up to a distant snow ridge. Further to the right again a group of mountains to the south of Keylang showed silhouetted against the light of the declining sun. Behind me there was only a snow slope leading up to an uninteresting ridge while to the west, though the mountains in all their glory, they were so covered in snow as to appear monotonous. I never got a really exciting view far up the valley for the reason that the mountains, though large and abrupt, were always flattened by the light.

I sat there for some time lapping it all up, until I got so cold that I had to run down to the village again. There I found that the coolies had arrived and on being told that they had been sacked wanted to be paid off so that they might make an early start, the first one they had even thought of making on this trip.

I then discovered that the ghorwalla[15] still wanted some details of the 'bandobast' settled so we went into conference again at length, and finally fixed everything. The coolies were then paid off with Rs25 against Rs21 earned and seemed pleased enough with it though I don't think that one of

14 Ruse.

15 Used to refer to the owner of the pony.

them understood the basis on which they were being paid. They were apparently surprised by it as they thought that I was very annoyed with them. I was, but I could hardly avoid paying them.

Down here it was warm in the day, if there was no breeze, but at night it was still chilly and I used to climb into all my trousers though there was still a large reserve of upper wear which was never forced into service even in camp.

In the morning we were off by half past eight on the road to Keylang. This wanders round the back of another village and then descends along the top of their fields nearly to the river where it enters a narrow portion of the valley. From there it climbs up along the side of a steep, loose hill avoiding an even steeper cliff down by the river. Opposite is an especially neat village set in a copse of fir which gives it the appearance of being misplaced in their barren land. These villages look most attractive from afar as the fields are a chequer of green with here and there a chorten[16] while the village close cluttered in the centre is an austere geometric brown, life being given to the scene by the black dots which are the villagers or their animals.

From its highest point the path turns to the north and follows the river down to it confluence with the Bhagat. Just on this corner there runs in from the south a nala which is said to be a way over to Bara Panagh. It was evident that even the most intrepid could not get over in May as the valley was then raked by avalanches and ended up in a steep snow and ice wall.

Coming down to the river again one gets the feeling of great spaciousness as the hills to the north of the valley lie back at a great distance from the road. Also at this height there is less snow to be seen as, though the south wall of the valley carries a lot, it is so steep that one cannot see the snow from down below. The rivers are not far off equal in size and the place where they meet is holy ground, there being a fine chorten built there in a grove of newly planted willows growing in the light grey sand brought down by the rivers. Passing this sanctuary we heard an awful din approaching and in time a procession hove in sight on the far bank of the Bhagat. We stopped to watch the form. Two drummers led the line, one man carrying a pair of drums and another following behind and beating. Then there were some pipes and at the back the god who was perched on the shoulders of a man, presumably the chief priest. Every now and again the party would stop and the god would be put on the ground while everyone marched round it twice with drums beating and colours flying. This was all very well until the drums went off without the sticks and nobody knew what to do. Arriving at the chorten they all marched round and round until they should have been giddy and then settled down to a sermon, so we pressed on.

Both rivers are spanned here by suspension bridges one of which we crossed and found on the other side that we had just four miles to go to Keylang. The road is mile posted for a hundred miles from Kulu but the trouble is that when they have a washout and a diversion near the beginning it puts the whole issue out of joint. They had evidently gone round measuring it again not so long before and they were nearly a mile out at Keylang. Which is all rather funny if you are not the PWD.

Just past the bridge there is one of the best willow plantations that I had seen and among the trees there were a mass of flowers. In general the flowers were rather disappointing though I think that some of the disappointment was due to the fact that I was early – but even so in this hard grazed country I doubt if one ever gets quite the superfluity of flowers to be found in the Alps.

The path runs along the west side of the river which has here cut a minor gorge. At one

16 A monument that often marks a mountain pass, often Buddhist.

point not content with enabling the traveller metaphorically to spit into the river it allows one to spit on to the opposite bank so steep has the snow been chiselled.

Emerging from the gorge one finds oneself in a wide shelf on which the village of Keylang stands, though at the other end. Impressively on a knoll on the other side of the river there is another village looking like a fortified town at the time of the crusades with its square brown houses clustered tight on the very highest point. One passes through yet another village and then comes into Keylang proper – or rather the official end of it. Keylang is two villages, in one of which the police and the doctor live and in the other is the dak bungalow. If one does not know it, it seems a long time from arriving in what they call Keylang and actually getting that cup of tea.

The bungalow has an excellent view as, while one cannot see either of the villages, one can see past them to the spectacular group of mountains to the south of the Chandra which show their best from here. Just opposite the mountain is rather dull as it is the reverse slope of the alp behind Gondla and has a level top though its left extremity abuts a truly fine mountain.

From the valley there is a definite line of approach to the first of these peaks but with the snow as it was the route was dangerous and, worse still, it would involve going right down to the river and up again in order to get to the foot of the climb – and the river was a long way down.

The afternoon tea was more than ever welcome this day as it had been distinctly hot in the sun coming up the last four miles from the Chandra. Within a month of midsummer, at about latitude 36 and at ten thousand feet the sun is remarkably strong even within reach of the snows – and worse still in the snows – and unless there is a breeze blowing one can feel oppressively hot. Yet so dry is it that one does not sweat noticeably however hard one is working. In the shade it is cool enough and that afternoon I was too cold sitting on the verandah and moved out into the sun of the lawn. I did not feel inspired to go for the evening constitutional as the immediate surroundings were fields and the only direct way out was up a steep scrub covered slope behind the bungalow. I imagine that this valley looks rather like parts of Provence only with the snows brought nearer, as while the fields are brilliant green a lot of the country is covered in firs standing in a gravelly desolation, which contrast makes a nice mixture of deep sage green and glittering grey.

I was joined on the lawn by a Lahouli who had an exceptional amount of inquisitiveness even for his race. He was a travelled man as he himself had been down to Lahore while his son had been all the way to Calcutta. This in contrast to the ghorwalla who had only been as far as Dharmsala and the sirdar who had never been beyond Mandi – so the word railway meant nothing to him – a curious thought in 1951. This old man was engaged in pasturing his cows, but as this was an activity which needed but one minute in twenty he had a lot of time to find out all about this strange sahib who had come up the valley so early in the year. In the evening I had another visitor – one of the policemen on wireless duty. There were four of them who operated a link to Dharmsala though god knows what messages they had to pass. They were all from the plains and thought nothing to being posted to Lahoul for a year. I learnt from them that the mail cannot get through for some 4-5 months of the year and that there had been twenty feet of snow in the valley that winter. I gathered from others, though, that the people are only confined to their houses for about a month. They do not sweep the snow off the top regularly and it is amazing that more of the houses do not collapse with the weight of it – or maybe they do but if so I was not told about it.

Keylang bungalow was the only one I stopped at which had a supply of reading material and so I buried my nose in *Blackwoods* for 1910 finding it most amusing as so many of the stories were written by army officers in the Indian Army. One was about a trip to Chamba which seems to have been similarly frustrated by a late lying snow field.

In the morning we set off at a good hour for the next bungalow at Jispa. This is a long stage as the go round here being thirteen miles. For some way the road goes along the side of the valley at a more or less constant height above the river until it comes to a gorge – or rather a cliff, as on the other side of the river the slope is no more than ordinarily steep. This is a most fiercesome looking place but in fact the going is a lot easier than in less dramatic sites, far less so than at a nala just to the north of Keylang. There had been some doubt as to whether we would be able to get past this with the horse and one look at it the night before had convinced me that it was impossible, as I had seen a local going up the far side of the nala where there was obviously no path worthy of the name and his shadow on the hillside came so near to him that it seemed that there could be no room left for a load. It was otherwise, though in going through I really felt most apprehensive for the safety of my kit. Bertie – the horse – did fantastic things. The nala is cut in loose gravel and scree but in this land of no rain it had been hardened and crusted to a fairly firm surface. But in one or two places the gravel was still moving and the iceaxes were used to make some holds for Bertie while we shouted to some gaonwalas[17] above to stop heaving rocks down the side. They were not doing this to annoy but merely to construct those portions of their main irrigation channel which had been carried away in the winter. They had a lot of work to do and had to put the channel across places which looked quite impossible – and without the aid of pipes.

Bertie was quite the least worried about all these happenings and did not even panic when he got his load caught in a rock by the side of the path just as he was leaping a soft spot. Nothing disturbed his equanimity though I was making full use of the iceaxe and applying all faculties to the job of getting myself along.

Having passed this spectacular gorge we came to a fir clad area which was as dry as a bone, but made up for it by being permeated with the hot scent of some herbs not unlike sage. And one or two streams of the coolest water suitably spouted for ease of drinking.

Going along here we met the local PWD man returning to Keylang and a raging conversation broke out between him, his assistant and my servants. Up till now we had been going on rumour as to the state of the road, but here at last was information. And it was not good. Apparently at a place a little way beyond Jispa a bridge, dismantled for the winter, was being constructed and meanwhile traffic crossed by a snow bridge. This was in an area which was 'all snow'. Above that, on the way to the last bungalow at Patseo there was a lot of damage and again the whole place was all snow. The good man then stated that I of course would not want to go there. I may well have been very rude as I was heartily fed up with everybody from the booking clerk at Pathankot upwards implying that the snows were the last place I would like to go to. I wanted to get right in among them.

Be that as it may we had a long way to go to get to the bungalow at Jispa. Having climbed up through the firs the path begins to descend though it takes the opportunity of going up and down a lot in the process. On the other side of the river beneath some finely chiselled cliffs and nalas lay quite the neatest village we had seen, all laid out in plan as we looked down on it by at least a thousand feet. Even the chaps said that it was a good village though on what grounds I am not sure though it may have been that it had a particularly fine gompa in the cliffs to the left.

Coming round a corner the road brings one to a slightly more open stretch of the valley

17 Villager.

and within sight of the village of Kolang where another of the Thakur sahibs live in a large house overlooking such fields as there are. This particular notability is an officer in the Gurkas, variously a captain or a colonel. He is reputed to be an excellent fellow and my sirdar actually admitted that he was a good Lahouli there being none other of the race for whom he had any respect at all. His grandaughters lined the roof of the house to watch our caravan go past while the children in the school below all stopped work to look at the strange phenomenon. The English are rather thin on the ground these days and apparently worthy of prolonged scrutiny. From Kolang on there is a stretch of three miles or so straight up the bottom of the valley to the bungalow and one has as a carrot the sight of a fine mountain sitting plumb in the middle of the valley about three miles further still. To the left too there is a fine mountain whose ridge rises in giant snow clad steps to impossible heights. The river runs close to the east of the valley and there is only one house on that side, rising sheer to the snows or allowing only a thin strip of sage covered scrub to exist.

We plodded on rather dusty and getting hotter than was altogether desirable. One trouble was that I carried all that was valuable in my coat, together with all the things that I wanted on the march; the two categories together being quite a weight. So I could hardly jettison that item of clothing and the rest was minimal anyway.

While we were resting outside the village of Jispa one of the locals looking like Errol Flynn in one of his more exotic parts and carrying a plough came up, but promptly broke the spell by asking for a cigarette. These people are not so bad as the Tibetans we met in Sikkim when it comes to asking for baksheesh but all the same they are not averse to a bit of cadging.

The bungalow is a long way from the village and is situated on the edge of another dwarf fir forest – and miles from the water supply. He who sited these bungalows cannot ever have wanted to wash and must have drunk whisky only as they are without exception built as far as could be from the water – and this in a country where water is channelled to every field. No one seems to have thought of laying on a private channel to the bungalow.

In the evening I went for a walk up the valley in order to see round a tantalising corner. I saw round the corner and was rewarded with the sight of a fine snow mountain about a dozen miles off framed by the sides of the main valley. Just here three more or less equal nala meet in a large shingle area. The only nala in which there is no habitation is the main one which goes on up to the north. Instead it has the bungalow at Patseo and the main trade route to Lahabih and Tibet. There is a fair in Patseo in July when all the produce of the north is brought down for sale to India. Patseo is one of those names which I could never pronounce right until I had tried aloud three or four times. It is more or less Patsy-oo except that the 'P' is as near a 'B' as one can go without getting there.

Having seen what lay up the valley and having ascertained that there was no snow for two miles at least I turned sharply to the left and went straight up the hill. This was steep and composed of gravel and sage which made simple if energetic going. I went on till the thighs ached at the very thought of taking another step up. Short climbs are well rewarded here as the valleys are so deep cut that from them one can appreciate the full grandeur of the mountains.

From this point I turned to the south and did a descending traverse back to the track not far from the bungalow. This was enlivened by one or two scrambles over some ribs of rock, but was more often a slither down through a cloud of dust. That evening I was rash enough to order corned beef for dinner again and the effect was the same as in Kothi only it was delayed for an hour more so that I got even less sleep. In the morning the order was given for all the tins to be chucked out and all and sundry warned not to eat the stuff.

The plan was that the sirdar and I should do a reconnaissance up the valley to find out just how true the rumours of bad roads were. We set off full of confidence from the bungalow as all looked too easy and I had seen no damage the day before. For the first two miles the road goes straight up the valley until one comes round the bend and can see the full sweep of the river bed. Then for another two miles or so the road skirts the south side of the Darche Nala until the stream has been confined to a more or less fixed bed. At this point a bridge was being built by about thirty men. They had only got as far as building the stone piers and had not started sticking in the wooden joists. Just below this bridge there are four piers which were said to be the beginning of a permanent bridge which the authorities had not had the money to complete so they had to spend many hundreds of Rupees most years rebuilding the wooden bridge. However, it was possible to get on to the far bank, as about a couple of hundred yards further up-stream, there was a snow bridge which looked to the uninitiated as strong as could be desired. Anyway it was easy enough to cross and there was no tendency to take a deep breath and double. A little way further up again there was the remains of another snow bridge one half of which had been washed away and the remaining half of which was being supplemented by a bridge of two planks across a foaming gulf.

We crossed over and followed the path on round the north side of the Darche Nala. Here there are a few fields between the hillside and the shingle while the houses cluster together at a point overlooking both the Darche and the Bhagat. The path climbs up the hill ascending gradually for a mile or so. Half way along we stopped and hailed the chowkidar who lived in the hamlet on the east side of the Bhagat. As luck would have it he was wandering about his fields and heard us and rapidly climbed down to the river 300 ft below, across a snow bridge and up to us, who meanwhile enjoyed a long rest. He was quite definite that it was impossible to get a pony up to the bungalow, even if one did, he said, there would be great difficulty with the wood as there was so much snow around that it could hardly be picked up near the bungalow and he would not be able to bring it up from his village which was the normal procedure. He even went as far as to say that it would be difficult for coolies to get up to the bungalow with anything in the way of loads. But it was necessary that we saw for ourselves and so we continued the ascending traverse this time as a party of three. Before long we reached the summit and the life went out of my limbs. There was the valley before one with no mountains of any more than usual interest – except for a delicious but quite unattainable thing on the left which was seen to its best advantage from here. The path could be seen going on down to meet the river again maybe three miles on, while the bungalow was another three miles or so further round a slight corner to the left. If we went on we would have to come back by the same route and it would be up hill going. We had already passed many places where it would be impossible to take a horse. Almost every stream worthy of the name had wrecked the path depositing on it a mass of stones and earth and carving for itself a deep channel for itself in the middle of the debris. What possible reason was there for going on? It took me a long time to work up enthusiasm again – maybe one of the disadvantages of being the only sahib, if one's own driving force falters even for five minutes the whole show packs it in.

When we did get going we gave ourselves a target where we could go and come back in time to be in camp by a reasonable hour and then I set off at a cracking pace. It was just about the fastest thing I could do without running and within five minutes I was so well going that I could not have stopped even had I so wished. While the sirdar would have dropped behind if he had been alone, with the chowkidar he had to keep up appearances and so we went along more or less 'ek sath'[18] until, at the appointed place, I was called to a halt by a shout from behind. We could not see much new from the luncheon stone, the main impression being of jumbled desolation. Lower down the valley was often a desolation, but here it was desolation piled on desolation with more bare rock than ever and masses of snow piled in all the avalanche tracks. We stopped here some time and I pursued my enquiries as to the roads which lead to the north. I was fascinated by the story that the next nala to the east used to carry a path over into Spiti but that 'aj kal'[19] no one could go as there was too much snow. Later in the year when the snow was less what a temptation that would have been for me. The sirdar's knowledge of the Bara Unga Pass must have been of the same traditional nature, and it is amazing how much of this remains of them though now they seem more or less tied to the routes sanctified by the PWD. I wondered whether in the old days before the British Raj made straight the highways the people had had to take their goods by coolie rather than by pony or mule which is now the only form of transport that they consider. Then it might have been easier to get over these higher passes which are now considered too difficult.

If one goes on from Patseo one comes in six or seven miles to a place rejoicing in the name of Zingzingbar and from there one enters on the region of the Baralacha Pass. This must be a queer spot as from the map it looks as though it passes from the Chamba to the north whereas in fact the trade lies over from the Bhagat, only the Spiti direct trade going over and down the Chamba. I used to wonder why all the trade went round the triangle this way, forced by the rivers, but the reason must be that there is much more wood on the western leg of the triangle. Near the Baralacha La there is none of this vital commodity to be found and I gather that one eats biscuits for a couple of days. At the same time rumour had it that the grass up there is of excellent quality during the short summer and it is here that the flocks from the south come. But this time this was a forbidden land as it was far too early in the year even to attempt a raid into such fascinating territory. I fear that the same Spiti has been written rather deeply into my brain and that I will soon be making a trip there – or at least planning one. I had not realised before, that all this part of the world is so easily negotiable in the monsoon which does not affect it in the least – that rules out next year as a possibility as I cannot possibly leave Calcutta in the monsoon. Spiti I am told has only two acres of cultivated land – there are no bridges over the rivers and one has to wade– the people are alleged to be more co-operative than the Lahoulis – its staple trade is done in yaks and I have an affinity for yaks; they represent the part of the Himalayas which seem to fascinate me most and like me they thrive best at height. What better collection of enticements could there be. In due course we set foot for home but this time at a more sober pace as there was a long way to go before we could get that reviving cup of tea.

Opposite his village the chowkidar left us and took his steep way home. He had told us that there was an excellent snow bridge on the way and that horses could be taken over it. I therefore, thought that as we could not go up to Patseo we would go up that nala which leads up into the mountains to the west. From what we could see of it the going was easy enough and it seemed to go right to the heart of the matter. Back on the Darcha nala a lot of progress had been made on the bridge but there was even more to be done. Our snow bridge was still intact.

At the bungalow we started selling the idea of a further advance to the ghorwalla who was not

---

18 Together.

19 Nowadays.

impressed as he had been stuffed full of the local villagers' ideas of how impossible it was. However it was agreed that we would make the attempt to put a camp on to the opposite side of the Bhagat the next day.

We did try and we successfully got up to the site of the bridge despite one or two nasty bits of snow which, though they worried his master, did not worry Bertie unduly. But at the bridge there was bad news; the snow bridge which was so 'pucca' the night before had half collapsed in the night and one now definitely went across it at the run if one went across it all. For ourselves there was the snow and plank bridge a little upstream but this was clearly not for ponies. We gathered that even if we did succeed in getting the animal across now, the bridge would not be ready by the time we had to pass on the way back and after seeing one snow bridge so transformed by the waters of one night our confidence in the others was shaken.

They said that it was possible to get an unloaded horse up the south side of the Darche Nala to a higher bridge but I at the time did not have much faith. We were utterly stymied. After a pause for general gloom I decided to pitch camp at a spot about a hundred yards from the site of the bridge just clear of the snow. This was a stony sort of place, but was flat enough and had water laid on. From here one could go up any of the three nalas without wasting much time. It was as good a compromise as I thought could be found. The view was not startling though up the Darche Nala there were some exciting ridges – at least they were exciting from this angle, from higher up they were a bit formless. Opposite on the other side of the roaring river was a steep khud-side which prevented one seeing the two houses built on a ledge further up. It was there that the ghorwalla went to get the grass for Bertie. Bertie himself was provided with a ready made pen but according to the pundits what he needed was some fresh green grass so he had a tendency to be taken down the valley in the day to eat and to return at night. This arrangement was not approved by the management as it meant that unless the sirdar stayed in camp there was no one to see that the kit did not vanish. And though one might suppose that this was as near the end of the world as made no matter there was a surprising traffic on the road which passed within a few feet of our tent. After the repulse at the crossing I was at a loss for ideas as to what to do and so used the time more profitably drinking tea and watching the few birds that there were darting up and down the stream. This was very fine at this point, keeping up a steady roar all day and only varying the mass of grey rushing water with an occasional block of frozen snow knocked off from a snow bridge.

In the afternoon I set off at a cracking pace up the north bank of the stream. There was a good path though no obvious place for it to go, as while the stream was sizable, the valley was narrow. This path wanders round the hillside for a few feet above the stream for about three quarters of a mile until one comes to a broader spot where it comes down to a little meadow beside the main stream. The grass here is kept green by a copious flow of crystal clear water from a spring in the rocks at the back. To complete the scene, some yaks were feeding there. I thought at first that there was no sign of human habitation until I realised that a small maidan on the south bank at which I had been idly gazing for some time contained a house – so well do these houses blend with the landscape. This happened on more that one occasion after I had realised the unobtrusive character of their buildings. Indeed the more obvious sign of human habitation was the terracing of the fields.

I rested there for a few minutes then raced over a waste covered in stones and mud brought down by a flooding stream, coming to some fields at the top of which was another house beyond which again on the far side of the nala was a third. All this in the remotest of valleys which at the entrance gave no signs of all these riches.

It would be admitted that the dwellings were very poor indeed and must suffer badly in the winter, but for all that they were proper houses even with such a poor wood supply and such scruffy fields. I was looked upon with a weary amazement – life does not seem to pulse in this backwater. I went on this time contouring along some few hundred feet above the river as I was dying to see round the bend of the valley. As the path was so good I imagine there must have been yet another house around the corner – but it was not for me to see. I just managed to catch a glimpse of a mountain far away at the head of the valley when my watch said it was really time to get moving if I did not want to get caught by the dark. What a tantalising country to travel in – here was a perfectly negotiable valley going up at least ten miles from the main road – and that in itself was about 65 miles from the nearest car. To the south of the valley was a side nala which though steep in the first section seemed to level out to give on to a snow col of apparent ease leading where? Having no map I could only guess and long to find out. But I could do little about it as I was confined to my horse and even if I had had the coolies I am sure that I would not have been able to tempt them that far off the beaten as they have none of the light-heartedness of the Sherpa and would funk the unknown. Probably a party of one sahib and a couple of Sherpas and a horse would be the most mobile in this place though I suspect there would be difficulties in bringing a Sherpa, but it is possible that the tie of being nearly Tibetan would render them less foreigners than the Kulu men. The valleys do not rise rapidly – nothing like the rate of 3,000 ft a stage as in Sikkim – and that means that one can go a long way in to the midst of hills and still remain at a low level, though that is not so much an advantage as it might be with the wood line so much lower. The area of lesser known mountains is so vast that one could spend a month just trying to get to know the area with two days journey from a point like my camp on the Darche Nala.

However, it was time to return and skirting beneath the most dangerous of stone capped earth pillars I raced for home. Already the shadows were filling even the broad part of the valley and so all attention was given to getting a move on. I hoped that the snow bridge and plank which I had crossed was still there as otherwise I should have to go a long way up again to find the next bridge, though that one looked as though it would be good for another week at least. I got back in good time though what the time was I do not know as one day my watch had stopped so we ran on camp time thereafter. It was set by my idea that it got light about five and dark about seven thirty. We were ten minutes out on return to Manali.

The next day a trip was planned up the other nala – that going up to the west. This was the largest of the three in width and should offer little difficulty. The obstacle would be in getting to it as this meant going some way along the Patseo road and then turning down and crossing the Bhagat before one even started on the journey proper.

We started off in fair time although setting off from camp was always slower than from a bungalow. We crossed the plank bridge and went down the north side of the stream until the time came to leave the main path for the way over the Bhagat. The locals had put up a bridge built on the same principles as the Sikkimese cane bridges but built out of twisted branches as they had no cane. This looked even less safe than a cane bridge and crossing it would have been rather fun. But the sirdar funked it and I was not sufficiently enthusiastic to try it by myself – the water below was very fast and cold. My opinion of the sirdar descended right to the bottom at that and I became convinced of what I had always thought before – that he was a poor mountain man. Instead of this we went up the stream for a few hundred yards and crossed on the snow bridge. From there it is a sharp pull up to the village on the ledge above.

I thought that so far I had seen some places, but this took the biscuit, being the most miserable of villages that I have ever seen. The whole thing was thoroughly unkempt, dirty and pungent. We had to ask the way here but there was no difficulty in that as the only thing of which there seemed to be plenty was the time of the able bodied men all of whom were lounging round the place shuddering at the thought of work.

The route went on round by an irrigation canal not yet cleared for the season and was defended by some thorns which showed an aggressive attitude towards bare knees. One of the disadvantages of the plan of tying the ends of the trousers beneath the feet and tucking the whole issue into the boots seemed to be that one's feet get so sweaty that they became sore. One had the strange phenomenon that the more one walked the more tender the feet became, so I took to shorts except on those days when I thought I would be going for long periods through the snow – it being most uncomfortable to get handfuls of wet snow down the turnups of the socks. Having traversed along beside this canal almost to the first tributary nala the path descended a bit and got mixed up in the scrub beside the river. The centre of the valley was a wilderness of shingle from which there rose on the north side a slope of gravelly scrub and on the south bare grass and snow. We stuck to the scrub and in so doing went up and down and in and out and around interminably. There was sort of a path but it was not continuous and most of the way was a sheep track. There were some herds pastured in the valley though there did not seem to be much for them to eat as all the herbage looked scorched even this early in the year. One thing was certain and that was that we ourselves were scorched, as this hill, at whose feet we were struggling, had small reserves of snow and cooling water was rare.

When at last I reached a spot where I could both eat and drink I stopped and waited an age for the sirdar to turn up. I was more than a bit annoyed for his being so far behind. We pressed on from there and once again the man showed his lack of mountain sense by taking a low route on one occasion when it was obvious to all and sundry that one would have to go higher a few yards later to avoid a particularly fierce bit of earth scarp. I left him miles behind on that move alone and so I set off independently across some steep going to what I thought would do as the turn round point. The view contained little fresh, but to get any further would have meant descending into and climbing out of a large nala with unduly steep sides, so I decided against. From here one could see that the main nala went on for another four or so miles where it divided into two, the main portion going round to the south, out of sight, while the straight forward leg led to the foot of an enticing mountain. About a mile in front of us a tributary came in from the left and it was interesting to see that while the main river was grey this stream was a rich brown colour, the two mingling to form a rather pale fawn mixture.

We sat here in the grilling heat for some time and I decided that it would have been great fun if we had been able to establish an advanced base somewhere up this nala as so many of the tributaries looked possible and they all led right into the heart of the mountains. However, it was not to be and we slid down to the river bed over a fierce scree which again left the sirdar standing and by the look on his face rather apprehensive as to what the sahib might do next.

What he did do was to turn down beside the river and make what progress he could over the boulders. This was an easier route by far than the high level one, but more dangerous as in many places it passed beneath massive cliffs of gravel which were definitely to be classed as 'unstable'. On the other side of the valley similar cliffs were rumbling away all the time. Also on the south side of this valley were a couple of houses in the most grim of situations, even worse than those up the Darche Nala, with their fields even now half covered in snow. What a world where summer does not come till June and the whole place is shut down again by October.

We made progress downwards until we came to one of the mill huts whose guardian was sound asleep in the doorway – we went in to see how it worked.

From there on it was easy going back to the village and then over the snow bridge and on to the main path. I was distinctly tired as it had been a trying day with never a long slope to go up or down, but always switching back from one grade to the other. Back at the bridge the work seemed to have made little progress – it having been a day of consolidation of the masonry abutments. My original plans had been made on the assumption that some food could be available locally, but it turned out to be otherwise. We had not bought anything other than a few potatoes in Keylang on the whole trip. So I was necessarily reduced to a rather desi diet which was based on rice and dhal for the evening. But I grew to like it and on those rare occasions when I allowed myself some European item in the menu it seemed out of place. The amount one can eat under these conditions is vast, my evening meal consisting of a large plate heaped as high as it could go with rice mixture – and boiled rice can go a long way.

The next day I planned an attack on the hill to the north of the Darche Nala. Looking at it I had come to the conclusion that not only was it easy but it was not so high as the others and so there was some chance of getting near the top of things – a fond delusion which would have been quickly dispelled if I had had a map with me, but I was glad that I had not. The sirdar claimed that he was sick and would not be able to come with me – his foot was sore. If you ask me he was so fed up with this sahib that he thought that he – the sahib – could go off and rush up and down mountains on his own.

Anyway in the morning I set off across the river alone. The second snow bridge was still in fair condition and looked good for a few more days and so I crossed it without much trepidation. From there I struck straight up the hillside and made good progress over the bare ground picking my way up between the tongues of snow as far as I could go. This being on the north side of the valley – the snow there was high, but such things must come to an end. On entering the snow I found that it was not so good. I was nearly always in to the ankle which is little disadvantage but often it was up to the thigh and in places up to the hips, which is no good at all. But by the aid of a zigzag course up the seeming hard bits and sharp diversions whenever one nosedived into the snow I was able to get on.

It was when crossing this snow that I saw the tracks of an Abominable Snow Man. What else could it have been? The signs were exactly right – footsteps in dead line ahead rather broader than they were long. I took some photographs of them, but they did not come out so no one will believe that they were there. That they were old, I admit, as they showed up as a change in the texture of the surface of the snow rather than as a dent in it. But they were definitely of the genus Snow Man Abominable. I pressed on.

Strangely enough towards the top the snow got softer rather than harder and I thought that I would never find a negotiable way up the last hundred feet. The view had been improving all the way up and when one came over the crest and could see to the north as well it was quite superb. Unfortunately there was some high cloud about, but at one time or another all the high peaks came out in their entirety. As one went up the proportion of snow in the landscape increased until at the top one could see little else. Also the mountains changed in value and that one which below had dominated the scene became of minor importance and vice versa. Unfortunately the only big fellow which did not clear was the group on the other side of the Bhagat which in the cloud gave the impression of hiding great surprises. To the north there was nothing of any great height to be seen though the ridge on which I was standing led up to a gorgeous abrupt thing which we had seen on the way up to Patseo. Here one realised that it was but the culmination of the ridge on which one stood and so there was no chance of reaching a proper top that day. Even at the point I had reached one could hardly claim that one had come to anything definite, so I tried to make a route up the ridge along which the going looked easy enough for some way except in so far as all the worst snow was on the ridge. Though it showed no sign of wanting to slip off it was equally determined that no progess should be allowed. Having wallowed up to my middle on two or three occasions, I gave it up as a bad job and sat down on a rock to eat my lunch.

It was there that I found the great virtue of raisins and snow. The former by themselves are apt to be a bit desiccating, but when well masticated with successive mouthfuls of snow the raisins are made to give up their full flavour and at the same time the thirst is quenched. It makes an excellent meal under the circumstances. After that, I set off down the hill and though I made good progress for a few hundred feet I got bogged down when trying to follow the tracks of this Snow Man off to the right. This particular soft patch was a large one and I was heartily fed up with the sight of snow before I escaped out of it on to hard snow and then on to thin snow where it did not matter if one did sink in as you could only sink in a short way.

Getting down an unknown slope is always more difficult than getting up it and I, out of perversity, chose a nala to descend. It started off in a reasonable form and provided a good path, but lower down it steepened to become little better than a gravel shoot, and at that one which in any other climate would have shot long ago. But the gods remained with me and progress was possible right to the bottom, so I never had to retreat or make a major diversion.

The gully came out some half mile or so above the yak pasture by the spring. From here on it was simple going and I took it leisurely as by then the slightly forbidding clouds of the morning had turned out to be the most magnificent of afternoons with enough breeze to turn the bright sun into an undiluted attraction.

The next downstream gully was in flood. It was eroding its course somewhere up the hill and the product was being rolled down the hill to the main river. I have never seen such a frightening aspect of erosion at work. As the stream came in sight over a scarp up on the hill, instead of being white or grey it was a rich chocolate brown consisting of stones in a liquid mud. This was all rolling down as fast as any flowing stream. On reaching the flatter ground the stream had spread out over a large area of the land, but always flowing in a channel six or eight feet wide between two foot banks of mud and stone. This channel with its banks was moving fast to and fro over the surface of the land leaving behind it a glassy waste. One could see new channels forming and old ones drying up even as one watched. At the edge of the main river where this stream flowed over an earth bank, I saw a new channel start, a two foot groove carved in the bank, and the stream dry up again all within three minutes. I was glad that it was not my pasture that was being so treated or for that matter that I did not live near a stream which might do this on one any day. After watching a flock of sheep cross the torrent apparently unimpressed by the change in its nature I set off for home, stopping to refresh myself at the spring on the way. From there on to the snow bridge I was followed by a character whom to judge from his hiccoughs had had an awful lot to drink. He bubbled away happily behind for most of the way and then started nattering away to me though I could not understand much of what he said. I think he was asking me if I had been to see his nala away on the other side of the Bhagat and if not, doing a spot of propaganda for it. Whatever it may have been he burbled on at great length until our roads were lucky enough to diverge. It seemed to be an even longer way back from the bridge to the camp and I arrived more than a little tired. I squatted down beside the fire and waited for the chae to come up.

Unfortunately along with the tea there arrived a party of Lahoulis who at the sight of a sahib in their midst promptly came over and set off on the eternal where have you come from, where are you going to questionnaire. They were sent away with a flea in their ear, and the sirdar explained that I was very tired and therefore did not want to talk to them just then. I have never seen men so amazed. These folk were on their way back from Kulu to their villages. In the winter they had loafed in the bazaar of Kulu and now that they thought that life was getting a bit easier up in the hills they returned to the land of their fathers where they would remain to do as little as they could until November when they would migrate back to the Kulu Valley.

What a contrast to the Scot of our own island who goes away to spend a lifetime on the Hooghly.

According to my schedule I should be on the way back the day after next to allow for one day at Keylang and another at Khoksar which seemed to be a fair way of breaking up the journey. But I had tried all the nalas and my one venture high into the snow had persuaded me that there was little future in that direction. So what to do? I decided on a complete day off and I have seldom succeeded so well.

If I had been able to take the sirdar on to the rocks with any confidence I should have made an attack on the cliffs directly behind the camp. These rose more or less sheer from a point about 300 ft above the stream and judging by a small reconnaissance I did one evening were of excellent rock. Though the upper parts would have had some snow on them they were so steep that it would not have been much and I think one would have been able to force a way up to the ridge. But it was not the sort of thing to do solo. On my day off the PWD people were putting the finishing touches to their bridge and I spent a lot of time just watching men at work. The hauling across of the final logs to bridge the gap between the two piers was a great work and accomplished without loss. The loss of a log in this place would be a disaster indeed as it would cost a lot to bring a replacement from the lands where trees grow that big. By the evening people were going to and fro across the bridge but it was still a feat of balancing and I gathered that it might be as much as four days before the thing was ready for normal traffic. And none too soon considering when the snow bridge had collapsed.

The next morning we made a good start after much exhortation of the ghorwalla. Even so there was some delay to commiserate with one of the locals whose pony had just died. Judging by the state of the fellow's other animal it died of plain starvation but it was described as a fever.

The stage down to Keylang was a long one, about 17 miles in all, and there had been some resistance to the idea that the horse could or would do it in one day. He did and in great form. The first move was down to the bungalow at Jispa where we had to pick up some kit and this was done before there was any chance of it getting hot. We had a short rest at the bungalow while the chowkidar came up to the village and got things organised. Thereafter we galloped down the valley which had become much greener and more lush in the few days that we had been higher up. In fact it looked almost a paradise in comparison.

I had been a bit apprehensive that it might be hot, but luck was with us and a breeze blew all day which made it most pleasant, combining the brightest of suns with a pleasant temperature. The road has been greatly improved everywhere and it was said by travellers that the nala to the north of Keylang was in good condition too. We passed a number of caravans of mules – very smart looking animals with elaborate halters and in some cases great tassels of red wool hanging from their necks. In this country it is only the horses and mules which carry bells, there being none on either sheep or cows or yaks. So these pack trains announced their presence by a merry jingle. Probably the idea is that thereby the ghorwallas of a caravan going in the opposite direction can whistle to their animals and tell them that there is something coming up the path and that there is no need for them to be frightened by it.

We got into Keylang in excellent time and after the vital cup of tea I went to have a look round the town. It was transformed while we had been away, the irrigation system had been put in order and everywhere there were babbling streams.

I found the chowkidar at work drawing in on his primitive hand loom. One day we had seen the preparation of the warp going on on a roof top. Two lines of pegs were placed at opposite ends of the roof and a woman walked to and fro hooking the thread over pegs at alternate ends. It must have taken a long time to do enough even for the narrow cloth they weave. It is amazing that these processes can continue in the face of competition from power looms – it is not as though the product is of such high quality that it could not be otherwise produced.

Later in the evening I went up the hill at the back of the bungalow and followed the fields out to that point where the channel was incut into the nala. In contrast to lower down the going here was quite easy and the channel did not appear to have needed repair for some time. The next day I thought that I would cross the nala to the north of the town again and then strike up the hill to see what could be found. There was in this region a fine two pronged mountain which I knew that I would not be able to climb, but I thought it would be amusing to have a closer look. I also thought it might be possible to contour to the south while up in the mountains and so rejoin the main path on the other side of the village. That was not to be, as the nala which is so steep by the road is as steep, though in a different way, higher up in the heart of the mountain.

I started in fine form as immediately after I had crossed the nala I struck off up the steepest of hillsides – and one almost devoid of vegetation except for a little scrub. In a few hundred feet I came to a house perched on a point overlooking the valley, proving that a Lahouli's home is his castle. Thereafter the slope eased off a bit and I edged my way up by the side of the fields until I entered an enormous area of dwarf fir forest – only this was not so dwarf as the trees were about 12 ft high. Coming out of that I turned off to the right and edged my way over the outer works of a snow field until I gained the edge of the next nala to the north. From this point a ridge led upwards to the tops.

As I came over the top and looked down into the nala I was greeted with a storm of falling stones and witnessed a deal of the far side of the nala falling down for no better reason than that it had been there too long. This continued for hours in a desultory sort of way and greatly added to the awesomeness of the ridge where it was happening – it started off by being a most fiercesome rock ridge anyway.

This ridge, and the one on which I was, appeared to lead up to the two pronged peak although there was so much cloud high up in the hills that one only caught an occasional glimpse of its full glory. My way was obvious enough as from me a ridge ran up curving to the left so as to end up overlooking the Keylang Nala from which ridge a large snow field sloped down to the right. This ridge was mostly of rock and provided a most interesting scramble though it was little more than that. It was made more fun by virtue of the fact that though one could escape to the right easily enough, to the left there was a sheer drop down to the scree below. Some way up I was brought to a halt by a change in the nature of the ridge as beyond that point it was snow and excessively soft. In any case it would not have been advisable to go on as the cloud level was not all that far above and I have no relish for being in a Himalayan cloud when I do not know the way and all around there is steep soft snow – I used it as an excuse to perch myself on a block and survey the scene. Even with the rather disappointing amount of cloud about it was superb. Long ago one had risen to such height as to be able to look over the ridge between Gondla and Keylang and see the full glory of the Shikar Beh ridge, this time shorn of its lower few thousand feet. To the south on the other side of the Chandra that group of mountains was looking at their best. They are good at all times though they are not inordinately high. But perhaps the best part of the whole thing was the view of the Keylang Valley in miniature. The thing was an indescribable green in startling contrast to the severe colouring of all the unirrigated ground. I took a colour picture of it later but even that misses the full quality of the scene. It was not too cold and by zipping up everything I was able to sit on my perch and lap it all up for quite some time. Descending was too easy and once off the rock I steered a bit to the north of my ascending course and on the way came across the most amazing display of a little pink flower whose name is not with me. It grew along the banks of an old channel which must have flowed undisturbed for a long time; the sight was such that I ran off the rest of the black and white film in the camera and put in a colour one.

Returning to the lower zones I found that it was hot but one was made to forget things like that by the sight of a gully on the other side of the main valley in the process of active erosion. As the stream in the Darche Valley was chewing up its path, so was this, but on double the scale. At the top of the gully a white stream entered and at the bottom, 500 ft lower, a vast chocolate torrent poured forth with a roar that could be distinguished even at this distance. And in the gully itself one could see the boulders falling down and being washed off to destruction. Nature at work on a terrifying scale. Erosion is something which one tends to think about as a slow and gradual process but here it was tearing the guts out of a mountain in broad daylight and at a rate of knots.

That evening the policeman and wireless man came up to see me again and complain about his lot.

The next day we made an early start as I wanted to get to Gondla early in order to get some pictures of the flowers out on the pasture behind the village. We also would avoid the heat to some extent if we were up from the lowlands before midday. We tramped off in great style and made excellent progress down to the Chandra though I was disappointed that I did not find more flowers worthy of being photographed in colour. Looking back I think that maybe it was luck as the pictures that I did take of flowers were far less striking than those of the ordinary things to be found in the valley. It seems that the colour which is in everything and is revealed by colour films is more arresting than the portrayal of colour in things which one expects to be coloured.

The chaps having valiantly pressed on without a halt for the best part of six miles at last came to the conclusion that this was too much of a good thing and stopped for a very long rest, in the most waterless spot they could find. Meantime I met the PWD man on his way back from a tour to Khoksar. He was most affable and I learnt all sorts of things from him beginning with the fact that the PWD did not start work in Lahoul until the 1st of May and stopped six months later.

Soon I arrived in the bungalow, and rather earlier than I thought likely the rest of the party turned up. I think that the ghorwalla was anxious to return to his home after so much travel in far places. After the inevitable tea I set off in gathering gloom for the hillside behind the village. Unfortunately the clouds came up fast and made a complete umbrella beneath which though it did not rain gave every sign of being just about to. The flowers had come on with the retreat – rapid – of the snows, but not quite to the extent that I had hoped. Even in the gloom though I could not resist taking one picture of them with the camera as open as could be.

I climbed up beside the stream until I reached the snow – or rather where the snow was continuous – and then bore off to the right towards the ridge which bounds the alp. I got about up to the level of the main ridge, though where I was the crest was a few hundred feet higher. By this time the cloud was touching the tip of the ridge at its western extremity and I used that as an excuse for going no higher, salving my conscience by noting that it was spotting with hail. I have a very healthy respect for cloud and rain in the Himalayas as on those occasions on which I have been subjected to either I have got thoroughly uncomfortable. These two dangers are not to be treated so lightly as they can be in the Lake District.

The whole afternoon's expedition was more in the nature of exercise than climbing as there was nothing much to be seen which had not been seen before and nothing much to do but climb up or down – and in that lay the joy, the joy of just existing in a perpendicular world.

Coming down I saw the site of a minor disaster where an irrigation channel had burst its banks and washed an awful lot of muck down the hillside. One must have to be on the watch all the time to see that all these streams behave themselves. I never found out for certain by what authority the water is turned off and on though in Keylang I saw a sort of guardian of the waters on patrol. The channels did not seem to be turned off and on at fixed hours of the day so maybe there is some piracy in the trade.

Back at the bungalow arrangements were made for an early start as, among other things, the PWD man had said that between Sissu and Gondla there were two nalas which had washed their bridges away and which might be difficult to cross late in the day. He said that we should start at five in the morning, but that hour is merely a way of saying that one should start early and seems to be interpreted as six by most of the chaps. We were all ready at six after an amazingly efficient preparation of food by the sirdar. For the first time he produced breakfast with the early tea and so made me work in double time for a bit. Needless to say the transport was late, but we were finally off by about a quarter past. We changed ghorwallas here as the father of the family wanted to go into Manali to buy his rations. That would make the housewives of Britain complain about the bus service.

We also added a second horse to the train although this was not to be at my expense. This was even more minute than Bertie and appropriately had a minute load. Bertie did not take well to the idea of being one of two and proved thoroughly obstreperous. He would not go as fast as the other nor did he take well to the idea to marching second. I think that he had had a good feed of barley the night before and was just averse to the idea of leaving home again.

We set out before the sun had reached the village and for some way it was chilly going, but as the cloud had gone away in the night the mountains were looking at their best. There was no sign of any fresh snow. We had not been going for more than an hour when Bertie took exception to a small clank from his load and dashed off down the path at a great speed and with such a motion that everything became untied and the rations were jettisoned – luckily into the road and not the river. We lost a bit of powdered milk, but nothing of any value.

After a few minutes all was lashed back and we set off again to overtake for the second time a vast train of donkeys. They were a strange crew and were apparently on their way to Manali with a few sheep to keep them company.

With amazing persistence we got all the way to Sissu without having a rest and did the eight miles in about three and a third hours which is definitely faster than the regulation two miles in an hour. The junior PWD man was at Sissu that day so there would be room at the Khoksar bungalow for us despite the fact that another party was ahead. We had received rumours of them at Gondla. They were a party from the Ministry of Finance. On the plain below Sissu we had a short rest and thereafter left the green area of Lahoul – or rather that area which has a few spots of green to offset the grey and brown. Higher up though a lot of the snow had gone, there was much less life to be seen. We came to the flooded nalas soon and found that there were easy enough to cross as we remained dry shod. After that things were taken at a more leisurely pace, but even so we arrived at the bungalow in seven and a half hours which is again in advance of the two miles in an hour schedule.

As I have said, a lot of the snow had gone but there remained substantial drifts to be crossed in places. Some work had been done on the road but as it was fair in the first place no great change was to be found. One bad thing though was that the melting snow had revealed one particularly high carcass of a cow which must have fallen off a very long time ago.

Standing around on the lawn by the bungalow was the group from the Ministry of Finance looking like a lot of hooded crows. I am afraid that I took no notice whatever and set about getting things organised as soon as may be. The road over the Rohtang was well used but in the middle of the day the snow was soft and so an early start on the day after next was indicated. That evening some clouds were coming up, but I, feeling that more exercise was needed, went up the path to North Khoksar intending the trip to be a reconnaissance for a trip to the Kulti Nala on the morrow. By the time I was crossing the enormous drift of old snow which lies to the west of the hamlet it was obvious that the cloud which was pouring over the Rohtang meant business and that if I went on I would get wet. I went on. What is a holiday if one does not get wet once in a while?

The path skirts round the edge of the fields which support the hamlet and then crosses the stream coming down from the Khoksar Nala by a snow bridge which looked to be on the point of collapse. I ran across it. Later in the year I think that a proper bridge is built there as this path is in good order except for those places where the hillside has slipped. It looked as though it had been made and maintained by the PWD until quite recent times and then left to the mercy of the elements so that though in all places possible for horses, it is only just so on some of the less stable slopes. I pressed on with all speed into gathering gloom. After I had been going for about an hour the rain began. It was neither hard nor cold so I continued and passed on the way the returning flocks of the village – cows, ponies, and sheep in that order. Never have I seen herds – boys and girls – more amazed at the sight of a stranger heading outwards on a grim evening. However foul the weather the trip would have been made worthwhile by the pink primulas which grew in clouds in the damper situations. They were by no means the only flowers in the place, but were possibly the most gorgeous of a lavish collection. The Kulti Nala makes a great sweep into the main valley and in the course of time has brought down so much moraine that the river is forced on to the south of the valley leaving on the north a desolate plain. Opposite I caught a glimpse of the path which we intended in the first place – and I was glad we hadn't, it looked like murder under the present conditions. The main valley further on was filled with cloud rack and gave no hope of a lifting of the weather which had by now become just a bit unpleasant. So I retreated behind a rock and prepared for battle by doing up all zips possible and getting out the hood of my jacket. As I was in shorts the nether regions had to look after themselves, but fortunately the rain was largely vertical and not much damage was done.

I then set out for home at full speed, really chasing over the ground with the thought of a cup of hot cocoa acting as the carrot. In the process I overtook the herd of sheep who were doing a slow movement act and again gave the fright of their young lives to the herds. By the time I had reached the hamlet of North Khoksar I was thoroughly wet and by the time I got to the bungalow just beginning to get cold. I had turned round at the crucial spot. But I was feeling better than ever before, a feeling which was accentuated by the thought of the babu log sitting and shivering in their blankets. I stripped right down to fundamentals – a rare process on these trips – and climbed into the sleeping bag to wait for the cocoa. I hoped that the rain would be over by the morning and enable me to press on with my plans. I realised that the rain would have had a bad effect on the snow already unsafe enough with the thawing. I woke up once or twice in the night and heard that it was still raining. I woke up in the morning and saw that it was still raining and quite hard enough to keep the most insane inside. I stayed in my sleeping bag.

Breakfast came, I stayed put and watched the spots come and go on the window pane. I developed an awful hunger and kept getting up and eating handfuls of raisins – which were still in good supply though most of the other items were on their last legs. I tried to work out the theory of three dimensional noughts and crosses, but came to the conclusion that Lahoul air was not designed for such things. I just lay in bed.

Lunch came and sometime later the babu log announced that they would like to meet me so I trudged in next door looking the greatest of ragamuffins, and talked to them for some time. They had come to do a survey of a village at the western end of the valley which had been picked out for the purpose of a random survey of agricultural finance. They came at this time of year because they had not quite realised how bad the roads would be. There were four of them and they had all come to do this work as they thought that whereas they normally went one at a time in this part they would need some moral support. They had crossed from Kothi not many days after myself and had thought the journey the worst possible.

They had gone down the valley and done their work in double quick time because they did not like the place. On the way back they had run out of food – they had brought over great sacks of atta[20] so that they might eat the food of their country for all the trip, but their calculation had gone wrong and they were left with insufficient supplies. They had tried the local grain, but did not like it. As they said so mournfully, 'they were filled with a nostalgia for home'! – they had no wireless to listen to, they thought it cold, they had none of the amenities of Delhi. I laughed like hell as here was I, not merely without a wireless, but without the food I usually eat, without anybody to talk to, after the sirdar and ghorwalla, unable to talk my own language, there for the pleasure of it – and loving every minute of it. The locals despised the babu log in a big way and were never so rude as about them. It would appear that they (the babus) tried to order them around and extort food from them, in neither of which attempts did they have any success. I was told that evening when it seemed doubtful whether anyone would be able to get over the next day that the rumour of the camp was that I would be able to cross the pass, but the babus would be quite stymied by it. I am

20 Wheat flour.

sure that I was no more of foreigner to the Lahoul than these people from the plains. The sirdar was always telling me how little he thought to the Hindu Raj and asking when I thought that the Grez log would be coming back. From his point of view the major factor was that the Hindu sahibs did not go in for shikar[21] and so his occupation more or less came to a standstill when the army left. I am afraid that all this talk made me most race conscious and full of the thought that it was a crime for people such as these to be ruled by the babus. Lahoul should really be ceded to Tibet. The Tibetans would not do much in the way of ruling it but I have yet to be convinced that the teaching of Hindi to the Lahoulis will do much good either. The babus were distressed to note that there were only three graduates in the whole of Lahoul. Knowing Indian graduates I should have said that it was perhaps the one hope for the place. If they forgot about teaching the people to write and spend their money on improving the quality of the grains they grow and of the roads they travel over, the ultimate benefit would be infinitely greater.

What the babus wanted to know from me was whether I was going to cross the pass on the morrow. Of course the answer was that I was going over in any event though I did add that I thought I might have a bit of a job persuading the ghorwalla to go. My resolution consoled them somewhat and they said that they would also go if I was moving – and this is 'their country'. They were all sitting round wrapped up in blankets and looking pictures of misery – to which picture a blanket draped round the shoulders and a rag tied over the ears are a sine qua non– I am sure that on their return to Delhi they will spin the most marvellous tales of the difficulties and dangers of the route but really they should be put on the mat for wasting the Government's time. One of them had to go direct to Delhi, but he had no intention of arriving there on the Monday morning as I had and also they had spent two days coming up from Gondla which is the easiest of double stages. However they boosted my morale no end by being so utterly wet.

During the day the ghorwalla came in and squatted down followed by the sirdar who did likewise. I guessed that something was afoot and that they had not come in just to warm themselves. It came out – the ghorwalla wanted to go home. These chaps may live in the mountains, but they are no end soft too. I said he was welcome to go if he provided another man to take the kit over to Manali on the following day. I owed him something of the order of fifty chips which I thought put him off for a bit as I did not really think that he would be able to recruit any other in that weather. Luckily enough I was right and the matter was forgotten about, he turning out in good order the next morning. His argument was that there was no food for the horses and so they would starve. And this despite the fact that we had brought up a sackful of stuff from Gondla and that he knew in advance that I was going to stay in Khoksar for a day.

I looked out of the window every now and again for any signs of the weather clearing, but always the rain came – until late in the evening, at about half past six, when I looked out rather perfunctorily expecting all to be as usual, but saw that the clouds had gone and a weak sun was shining into a pale washed out world. I went into action and putting on enough clothes to be decent sallied forth.

Firstly I made one or two trips round the camp and then gathering way set off to the other side of the river where a number of shepherds were encamped. They must have the most miserable time of it in this weather. We had met the first flock of sheep and goats to come over from the south somewhere between Gondla and Sissu and thereafter there were many. They were all from

21 Sport hunting.

the Kulu Valley, the parties from the Kangra Valley not having arrived as yet. Most of the flocks between Sissu and Khoksar were just sitting and recuperating from the long trek over the hills. As our ghorwalla said it means two days without food at this time of year and even on arrival the pasture was sparse in Lahoul with the spring being so late.

The tents in which these people live are little more than the area under the edge of the tarpaulin which they stretch over the central pile of sheep packs. The tent-dwellers looked very sorry for themselves indeed as they huddled round their meagre fires.

I did not go far in that direction as the ground was a bit rough for my own gym shoes, but on return to the other side I found that something had got into my blood, I could not stop moving, often finding it difficult to stop running. I dashed round and round the camp to the astonishment of all. But in so doing got a lot of the excess energy out of the system. Running flat out at 10,000 ft is an exhausting process to those who are in training only for plodding on and on at a steady two miles an hour. I rushed about till ten to eight when it had become so dark that I could not see where to put the feet. In the process I had told the babu log who had ventured out to take the evening air, that the next day's journey would now be too easy and all that it required would be an early start. How furious I was that this clearing of the weather had not come three hours earlier in which case I would have been able to make some sort of a day of it instead of just accumulating bumptiousness.

Even with such an idle programme behind me I slept soundly that night only to be woken up at an unearthly hour by the babu log next door. The previous day they had a sing song in which they made the most mournful of noises which I imagine were poignant outpourings of what a grim place they were in, but this chatter in the small hours was even more annoying. I remained firmly in bed for another three quarters of an hour after they commenced frolicking around like boys on the last day of term.

Breakfast came with the tea and a quarter of an hour later I was more or less organised. This time the ghorwalla was ready too and we set off within five minutes of six o'clock. The babus set off at the same time wrapped in their shawls and with polas on their feet but without their transport which was taking a most philosophic view of life. Their man was taking a dozen mules into Manali although the kit only accounted for two.

The babus pressed on at a terrific pace and were soon miles ahead as I plodded along in the cold dawn with the ponies. The track was good except that at this hour the snow was so hard and glazed that the snow drifts were difficult for the animals, but they had a fine technique of edging in to combat the ice. It did not seem to worry them at all. By the time the sun reached us we had got on to the steep portion and we looped up in great zigzags to reach the scarp at a point far different from our outward route. There the babus were congregated frightfully proud of the fact that they had got there first, but looking more than ever out of place with a vast snow field as background. On the upper plateau there had been a heavy fall of new snow through which one could just trace the old track. The snow would in general not quite take one's weight though I noticed that the locals, whether because of their foot wear or the way they walked or because of their weight did not sink in as far as I did. I developed a shuffle which helped, but even so I sank more often than they did.

I pressed on at a good pace exulting in the clear morning air and the bright sun on clean snow, reaching the top some way ahead of all the rest except for one fellow who was determined that no sahib would get the better of him and who hung on to the last minute. At the top I took a round of photographs and took a long last gaze at the glorious mountains of Lahoul which were looking better than ever after their dusting with new snow. Actually they must have been not a little unsafe as the nearer slopes which we could see in detail were scarred with many small new avalanches. That together with that the snow was rapidly softening put me off the idea of going any higher than the top of the pass. In most conditions it would be easy going to climb another 2,000 ft to the top of one of the flanking hills but then one would have been up to ones middle in snow before the day was much older.

The horses turned up on the heels of the babus and were making magnificent progress considering that their small hooves were sinking in about a foot at every step. They had an excellent technique of putting the rear hoof in the hole which the fore hoof was at that moment leaving. It looked most unstable.

After getting the sirdar to record my beard in celluloid, I pressed on intent on getting as far down as may be before the snow got really soft. We had climbed the pass in two hours twenty minutes. Going downhill was just a matter of putting one foot in front the other and letting the snow do the braking for one so we were down at the nala in no time. There the path was free of snow and had lost a lot of its terror – but to compensate the body of a donkey was spreadeagled on the snow below. The death rate among animals in this must be immense – in Khoksar we were told of a donkey which had been bitten to death by another one the afternoon we were there.

Beside the path going round that nala were some of the most glorious of primula – not so delicate as the pink fellows met with elsewhere but more flamboyant. The sirdar picked a bunch for me which I zipped into my pockets, and stuck into my hat.

A little further down a halt was called at a water point and I had some of their chuppattis with my raisins. It was rather pleasant having potato and something hot added to the normal atta.[22] We were by now out of the snow – the snow line hardly extended below the nala – and progress was excellent. We met a civilised Indian couple coming up on their way over for a day or two in Lahoul and I realised by their well disguised looks what a curious character I must look.

I chatted for some time with them and then set out at a rapid pace for the bungalow. In the process I overtook all the rest and got horribly hot – I really felt that the Kulu Valley must be a grim place if it was so warm even at this height. The reason I think was that it was wetter than the Lahoul Valley and I began to sweat more freely on crossing the pass.

But the flowers down by the Rahla bungalow were magnificent. Not that I noticed anything of great individual beauty, but the whole place had blossomed forth into a mass of blooms. The only thing which had disappeared was the primula Wanda which grew on one side of the stream, but which was now overgrown with weeds.

The bungalow was open, though the chowkidar got me annoyed almost straight away by getting on about this pass question gain. He thought he was on a good one when the rogue offered me fried eggs which he knew well were a rarity in Lahoul, but I preferred to finish my supplies of the raisins. The trip over the pass took just five and a half hours which was not bad going and shows that it would be easily possible to get down to Manali in one day from Khoksar. Thus according to my reckoning if one really wants to go to town one can do the trip from Keylang to Manali in two days, but they would both be hard ones. The sirdar was not as long coming as one might think and he was followed in six and a half hours by the ponies who had done a magnificent day's work. The babu log did not turn up for hours. Afterwards they told me that though not as bad as the trip over

22 Wheat flour used for bread.

they still found it most tiring and unpleasant.

After the usual tea I started off into the jangal[23] which abuts on to the bungalow. One has to cross a field or two and then the forest is around one – and here it starts off at an incredible angle. One climbs up the first few hundred feet in just about no distance at all. There was some sort of a path to be found though it was vague and had bits missing from it here and there. However, by the time I had climbed up for a few minutes I came to a proper path which bore off to the left climbing all the way. This was obviously used a great deal as there were many hoof marks on it. I toiled up to a pasture land on a broad spur above the forest. The pasture began in tongues leading down into the forest and gradually spread out so as to occupy the whole spur leaving the trees to make do with the nalas. It was a delightful alp though there was even less grass and more flowers than in most of Switzerland. The chief joy at this time was a thing like a wild strawberry flower, but which had its blooms in white blue or yellow, that and of course the iris. In Lahoul this iris has the status of a weed and all the pastures are covered with its green blades and brilliant blue flowers.

The path became indistinct as it entered the grassland, but it held out long enough to take me to a place from which I could see a cairn standing beckoning at the top of the ridge. I allowed it to beckon and arrived at this vantage point just as it was beginning to rain – or more strictly to hail. I crouched down in what I thought was the lea of the cairn, but as it was scarcely as wide as myself hardly succeeded in keeping much of the muck off. But by virtue of doing up all the crannies of my clothing I was able to keep warm enough. Though there was a deal of cloud about which obscured the view this was definitely an excellent place from which to survey the top end of the Kulu Valley which was all laid out before me as for inspection. By analogy and such reading of the map as was possible I reckoned I was rather better than 12,000 ft up.

This particular ridge was remarkably free from snow though there was not much to eat for the ponies who were wandering about on it. To the south there was a ridge of dirty snow dividing us from the Hampta Valley, but that was enclosed for the most part in even dirtier cloud within the outskirts with which I was now involved. In the middle of it would have been really unpleasant as the hail stones were by no means small. The most distinguished of the aspects was up the Solang mala most of whose bounding ridge was in sunlight though the major peaks were well wrapped up. The map marks a path out of the nala on the way to Bara Banaghal but from what one can see of it from here the way must be difficult indeed as the terminal wall looks as near to sheer as it could reasonably be.

To the south it was murky and the hills were undistinguished when seen from this altitude though from lower down they effectively dominate the scene.

At length I decided that I had better be going down if I thought to be home in reasonable time. The path was one of those which are so steep and continuous that there is no rest for the thighs whatever and I was tired indeed when I reached the bottom. Fortunately I arrived in more or less the right place as on the way down I completely lost my climbing route and went down by guesswork. These great forests are most confusing as though they are not very dense one tree growing to a hundred feet looks much like another.

Though I could not get this confirmed by the sirdar it seemed to me that they made charcoal in the forests as well as collecting their firewood from them. Many of the tree stumps were charred and I had the impression that they chose their tree, cut off the bark round the base, allowed it to die,

23 Forest.

and then fired it to give them charcoal. They are quite unable to cope with the larger trees when they crash to the ground and the forest abounds in hulking monsters lying flat on the floor with their minor branches hacked off and only a few feeble attempts made on the trunk. Even if one did succeed in cutting a bit off the trunk one would have such a time getting the thing down to the village below that it is undoubtedly easier to confine one's activities to the smaller branches.

Back in the bungalow I just lazed around for the little more time that remained and made vague attempts to arrange things the way I would want them on the journey down to the plains. I drunk more mugs of cocoa than I like to remember – we had bought some more sugar from the chowkidar – sugar being the one thing which had run short, or rather the one vital thing. I had been eating the stuff at a rate of two pounds a week, and all that in drinks of one kind and another – mostly the great standby, tea. We were due to set off at eight in the morning as I wanted to have a bit of time down in Manali to get things finally organised. Actually we set off a bit before as the morning procedure had been well learnt by all. The babus were mooning around in rather an ineffective manner, being due to go to Manali also but they were to spend the night in the bungalow there and not go on down that day. I had not seen them the night before as one of the first things which the sirdar had done on arrival in the bungalow was to bolt the door leading from my room into the main room. I was definitely not to be allowed to have more than formal intercourse with them.

We made good time down to Manali though I was going in my shoes and was heartily fed up with them by the time I arrived. There had been many flocks of sheep and goats going up the valley before we set off, apparently to spend the day near Rahla before crossing the pass. All these were sheep from the Kulu Valley, but just about a mile from Kothi we came across the first of the Guddi log – the people from the Kangra who to me are distinguished by the fact that they wear short pants and their tunic is much fuller below the waist than that of the Kulu people. I first thought that there was something to do with the wearing of earrings and other decorations but enquiry proved the system I was evolving to be false. The Kulu women go in for a lot of rings in their noses, extravagant necklaces and a whole earful of small rings not so much in the lobe as higher up. These often so bear down the ear that it droops forward. The Lahoul women have an entirely different system of decoration as befits the fact that they are more Tibetan. The main idea is that the hair is parted down the middle and drawn smoothly back on each side. Forward of the temples are placed smooth flattened balls of polished wood which are connected to a decorated plate worn on the back of the head. Plate seems a bit uncomplimentary but it is the only word I can think, of being an embossed ornamental disc about three inches across. It is usually made of silver. From the cord which runs from the plate to the globes hang plaits of yak hair.

An alternative idea more prevalent among the older women is to have a thing like a great fur cap with the back missing. The sides come right down on the shoulders and are then pinned back to meet above the crown while down the back, covering the nape of the neck, is a bit of cloth with a number of baubles sewn into it.

The weather was determined to have the last say in the matter and about half way down we ran into a shower of rain which luckily was very short lived, but wet enough while it did.

A bit farther on we met another long caravan of sheep – this time all from the Kangra. They stretched for about a mile in a continuous Band about six deep on the path with their shepherds here and there trying to keep the flock intact. Some of them had succeeded in separating the sheep from the goats and the goats would lead the band looking very fine in their long white coats and curving horns while behind would be the more prosaic sheep. Last of all would be one or two of the kids being carried along. I imagine that these only get preferential treatment for four days or so as some minute things were rushing along with their mothers. It is a wonder that the whole lot do not die of exhaustion when being taken through the snow, though the adult animals looked very fit considering that they had travelled over a hundred miles at the very least already.

Manali was looking like a metropolis and there were a disconcerting number of the sahib log about. I had hardly settled down on the verandah of the bungalow and was getting things organised in the way of paying off the boys when a half colonel turned up to be quickly followed by some other miscellaneous characters staying in the bungalow. The place had become popular in the three weeks I had been away.

The first thing was to get a barber to remove the beard which he did efficiently though not with that deliciously smooth result there should have been. I nearly told him to keep the moustache on as that was by far the most painful part of the operation – maybe because he had left it to the last and by then the razor was blunt. It is quite essential to have a barber on this job as removing it by a safety razor would be sheer hell.

After that I had to make sure that I had a place on the bus, but as it was the turn of the Kulu valley company to run the thing no one was to be found who knew what went on.

So I went up to the Hotel, as it is grandly known, and found out that they had made the arrangements and also that there was some mail waiting for me. Two letters from Cambridge and a *Punch*. On what system they sent them up to me I do not know, but the Punch was the best thing they could have thought of and I read the thing from cover to cover many times and thought it funnier every time. Sure enough in the fullness of time the driver of the bus turned up and they knew about me. So the luggage was piled on and I was installed in the front seat. We started, only to stop a hundred yards farther down while some other problem was sorted out. I then discovered that this bus only went as far as Kulu, from then on the service being run by the Government. I thought that was a good thing from the point of view of comfort, but it was obvious that the booking arrangements had only been made as far as Kulu so I still had pictures of arriving well behind schedule.

We left Manali. The road was not in too bad a condition though I gathered that on the other side of Kulu it had been closed for six days by a washout which one had to walk across. They had had a lot of rain in the last few days and I was lucky indeed to have been away in the rainless Lahoul Valley. We trundled down to Kulu with the mountains gradually showing themselves less often as the journey to the plains got under way. At one point the bus decided to stall as the petrol had run out – or rather the boys could not fiddle quite as much as they had hoped to. So for ten minutes we were stranded in the most difficult of places where one got out on the near side only to drop down the khud-side to the river.

Major Banon was in Kulu in his ancient Morris and we exchanged compliments – holding the bus up for some time in the process. We then moved on for another quarter of a mile when a car passed going up carrying the most pallid of European women that I have ever seen. Most important was that the road was now through so we returned to the bus depot and got down. Soon the other bus turned up and a little later we had all got tickets and the whole party moved off. At the other end of Kulu a whole host of local bigwigs got on including one who by his hearty manner and habit of taking all and sundry off to have a secret talk, I thought must be the local political boss.

As he told me the next day he was the MLA for Kulu – the Thakur Sahib in fact. So he must have jumped onto the band wagon at the right moment and donned the white cap. He was on his way to Simla for that row which forced the Chief Minister to resign, and Governor's rule to commence. He was not altogether a foolish fellow as he told me that on his annual tour into Lahoul which is also in his constituency, he always started drinking the local brew on arrival in Khoksar and did not leave off until he crossed the Rohtang on his way back.

We rattled our way down the valley to Aut where there was another short rest and then through the gorges in the shadow of the setting sun. The sun was dead ahead in those places where the road climbed up in a westward direction and I, sitting beside the driver could not see a thing. This with a cliff up on one side of the road and down the other, did not seem a good thing.

The country below Pandoh looked more attractive than on the way up with gentle clouds floating in a rain washed sky and the surrounding jungle looking clean and fresh and not hidden under a mass of dust as it had seemed to be before. We ran into Mandi more or less on time. I was then surrounded by a host of hotel keepers. I could not face the idea of an hotel in this filthy town so I tried to persuade the bus authorities to let me sleep on the bench in their waiting room. I was successful though they were very apologetic as to the state of the place. The fellow who thought he was on to a good thing brought along a charpoy so I was well set up for the night. First though I went out to get hold of some tea as I was parched. It was a horrible brew, but it did the necessary. I found that I was still antipathetic to the town of Mandi – in fact possibly more so as though it seemed less filthy than on the way up, it seemed at the same time far more akin to the plains than to the hills. I wandered here and there but got so fed up with being stared at that I retired to bed though the din of the bazaar outside the door continued for some time. I slept soundly enough until three o'clock in the morning when I was awakened by a procession of women passing the door chanting some hymn. Then at a quarter to four the chowkidar started rousing the company though the bus did not leave until five. He was very effective and once he had started there was no point in trying to sleep on, so I gave it up and went out into the fresh and not too warm air of the morning. Long before the scheduled time the bus was waiting ready to go off with a more than full complement of passengers. The delays in getting the driver sorted out and filling in all the forms were endless and it was dead on five when we left. Dawn had broken – though not peacefully as while we were waiting in the market square another procession of wailing women had gone by with a number of powerful lorries dashing off into the night to compete. The object of all this motor activity is to coincide with the one way timings on the road to Jogindernagar. It is an amusing enough road though the knowledge that one was on the way back to work and the fact that one had started at an early hour mitigated any tendency to enthusiasm. The one thing which really struck home was a view of the hills behind Dharmsala with just a little snow left on their tops silhouetted against the morning sky. They were small and far away but they were the last mountains that would be seen for a long time and they were placed in a perfect setting.

At Jogindernagar we stopped for the ritual cup of tea though there was nothing to go with it such as would make the stop worthy of the name of breakfast. After that it began to get hot, Baijnath was warm, Palampur was cooler being up the hill again, Nagrota was warmer and by the time we had got down to Pathankote it was hot – over 100° I should think.

From Nagrota on the road is an excellent one which to judge from the dates of the bridges was started in the 1880s and has been improved ever since, largely one imagines at the insistence of the army. Disappointingly enough one neither goes through Kangra or Dharmsala, but steers a middle course between them keeping a more or less straight line for the plains. For twenty miles or so from Nagrota one goes through an agricultural land which is plainly extremely fertile, but, then one drops down through the dry scrub forest which is so noticeable from the train. This wilderness stretches almost all the way down to Pathankote and seems to support very little in the way of life – in fact police stations would seem to be one of the main activities. The buses running along this route have to stop every now and again to report to the local fauna. Just outside Pathankote where the other road comes in there is a major check point where we were parked out in the boiling sun for the best part of ten minutes.

Once we had passed Jogindernagar the whole company which had been chattering away like a monkey house up till then fell asleep with the one exception of a young fellow chaperoning his sister down to the plains who was most abominably sick. The journey must have been hell for him as the bus swings about and bumps around all the way never having a straight and smooth stretch in which to gather poise. Luckily the rest of the company remained quiet until they were decanted in the station yard at Pathankote long before due time.

I had four and a half hours to waste. I had a lunch which was almost as horrid a meal as on the way up, but I was conditioned to try it now. I bought a paper but almost threw it away in disgust as the world seemed to be having exactly the same troubles as when I left it. About five o'clock I got into the train and found that I had been given a coupe with a man in the MES who was due to get out at an appalling hour of the night at Amballa. He had been on a tour up in the hills and was full of curiosity as to my doings and particularly as to how I had managed to stand it going by myself. It was hot but cooling rapidly as we meandered down to Amritsar. We arrived there in the dusk and I opted for an Indian meal as I thought that it could not be worse than the so called European food I had had at Pathankote. It was not and after I had eliminated one or two things which were not so good I was left with an excellent feed – which would have been better still if eating it was not such a messy process.

We got away on time and soon it was cold enough to clamber under a blanket. I vaguely remember something happening in the middle of the night when the other half got out, but I really came to life when I leaned down and looking out found that we were only thirty miles from Delhi.

I climbed down and engaged in the most monumental of washes. I learnt that if one really sets about it it is possible to get a deal of dirt off even in an Indian train. I packed everything up and left off putting on my one and only clean set of whites – which had trundled round all the way in the end of my bedding roll – until we were just running into Delhi station. It was 7.45, we were dead on time and it was not hot yet. I took a taxi round to Maidan's and found that no accommodation had been arranged for me. I had a long cool bath in which another layer of the dirt was removed. I then startled the staff by the amount of breakfast I could consume. Taking a taxi to ICI's office I discovered that I was to stay with the boss there.

Two pleasantly idle days in Delhi which though hot was by no means grimly so, and then away by Viking back to Calcutta. For the first three hours it was as smooth as anything and then we were flung around all over the place, but luckily I had remembered to take the pills and the breakfast kept in place though I could hardly claim to enjoy the process. Calcutta was sticky.

Comparisons with the trip to Sikkim seem to be indicated, but it would be as easy to compare the hills of Skye with Cross Fell. Though both Sikkim and Lahoul are in the range we know as the Himalayas, the connection between the two areas is valid only for one viewing them from such a distance that no detail is discernable and to whom the Himalayas are fully defined by that one word.

The whole set up is different. For one thing being further to the north the tree level in Kulu is lower – two or three thousand feet lower than in Sikkim. For another the rivers do not cut down so sharply as the Tista which descends from its source at 18,000 ft to the plains of Bengal in less than 100 miles. These rivers usually only drop at a thousand feet in a stage – not always that fast. The people too are wildly different having a different agricultural background as their setting. Yaks in Sikkim are the main transport animals of the way over to Tibet. In Lahoul the idea of using a yak to carry anything never occurs to them. But the greater difference between the two trips lies in the fact that on this latter I went alone and on the former I had a European companion. It is not really true to say that I went alone as with me were the rest of the caravan and all the local characters who were usually only too pleased to exchange a word or two. On balance I prefer the second alternative as one is then cut off from that civilisation which is Calcutta and if one thinks about it at all – as one necessarily does – it is entirely of one's own volition. I was a bit apprehensive when I set out that I would get rapidly fed up with speaking Hindi all the while. I was gratified to find that that did not irritate at all, and though my vocabulary was very limited it was sufficient to carry on day to day business and to find out a deal about what goes on in that part of the world. By leaving behind so much of what is normal in Calcutta and taking with one no books or companions to remind one of it, I think one necessarily enters more fully into the life of the country in which one travels. And though I would be the first to say that talk of living with the people and really getting to know them is a lot of high sounding waffle I find myself thinking a modified form of this waffle. I would not claim that I in any way became a Lahouli but I do think that I found some of the problems which attach to their way of life – and though while in Sikkim we also found out a lot of what went on there I feel that I found out rather more in Lahoul. Is that an advantage? I would not like to dogmatise, but I find that it is a satisfaction and one is always at liberty to say that one has broadened the mind thereby.

Naturally I learnt a deal more about travelling in the Himalayas and travelling under very different conditions than in Sikkim. For one thing the snow was 8,000 ft lower and for another the roads were built in a manner which would not last five minutes in the rain of Sikkim. I know now that some things which I left out of my kit as I thought that they were unnecessary were really useful while others like a tin opener were superfluous. More important I lived for breakfast. I got to like it and in future will certainly go equipped for eating in that style rather than going to all the trouble of lugging along vast quantities of food in tins to enable one to eat in the European style. One has to develop a stomach which can cope with such a vast quantity but once that is done there is no trouble to be found in feeding as the chaps can eat just about what one eats oneself, except that to take enough sugar to feed all at the rate which I consumed the stuff would be nearest to impossibility. Photographically the results were very mixed as, while the black and white were thoroughly bad, the colour were quite good – and it is the colour ones which show just what a glorious country it all is. Actually the ones of flowers are not so good as those of the scenery in general as in the latter case the use of colour seems to bring out the contrasts in it whilst the flowers seem very ordinary though in the flesh they are startling.

I have come to the conclusion that I will never make anything of a Himalyan climber as I am always far too keen on seeing round the corner—and there is always a corner round which has not been inspected before. To ascend a mountain—even a small one—needs the tactics of a siege and my impetuousness will most often lead me to abandon that and move camp round the spur to have a look at what happens the other side. Usually one can get a good idea of the layout without going to the top of the main peak – the side ones giving fine view points. For that reason I come back full of ideas as to where to go next rather than with any scheme to attack a particular mountain. My plans are not so prolific as they might be as I now realise that one must go to the land of the yak not earlier than the end of June or July. And it is to the land of the yak that I want to go. In brief I should like to take a horse and a sirdar and camp my way round all that part of the world which lies north of the Great Himalaya and within a hundred miles or so either side of Keylang. There is not great difficulty in travelling in this area nor are the mountains as spectacular as they are in many other places in the Himalayas, but for me the project has the advantage of being akin to travelling in Tibet without the political complications attendant on the real thing. Why Tibet should have such a fascination is more than I can say – but it has one almost rivalling Samarkhand and Bokhara, those magic names whose silks and carpets seen in shops bring home to one that the bazaar in Calcutta is vitally connected with the East and is not merely a dirty outpost of our own Western civilization.

House in the bazaar at Pathankote

Mandi: the bazaar

Bridge over the River Beas

A temple in the garden of the main square

A hamlet on the road to Kothi

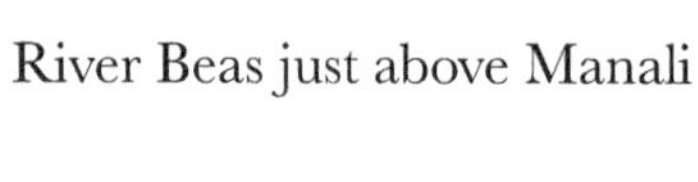

River Beas just above Manali

Barley fields above Manali

Deserted dak bungalow at Rahla

The River Beas

Manali
Sheep in the Bazaar

Flocks of sheep and goats on trek

By air

By pony

By bus

By train

And by coolie

The coolies messing about before setting off for the Rohtang

and actually setting off

and taking the first of many rests

Coolies at work on the way up to the Rohtang Pass

And as they more usually appeared

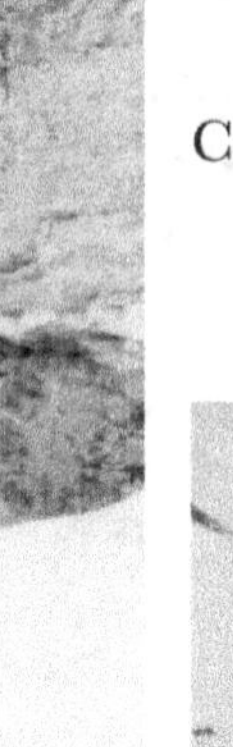

Cow on its way over the Rohtang Pass

Cuttting the path over the Rohtang (May 16th)

The new bridge over the Darche Nala

Blossom in Keylang

A stream of mud helps to erode the Darche Nala

Opposite Keylang a stream enters a gully white and emerges brown carrying with it a mass of mud and stones

Yaks busy ploughing at Gondla

A view of North Khoksar from the Rohtang path

A Lahoul skyscraper at Gondla

A group of houses above Gondla

Thakur sahib's house at Kolang

Religious procession at the junction of the Chamba and the Bhagat

The chorten to which they were going

On the road up to Keylang

He who thought it was worth Rs1,100

The sirdar

The chowkidar of the bungalow at Kispa

Fish out of water—babus from the Ministry of Finance on the march

Breasting the summit of the Rohtang

Characters met on the wayside between Sissu and Gondla

Children at the bungalow at Jispa

and the most inquisitive of the bunch

Looking towards the Rohtang Pass from the South

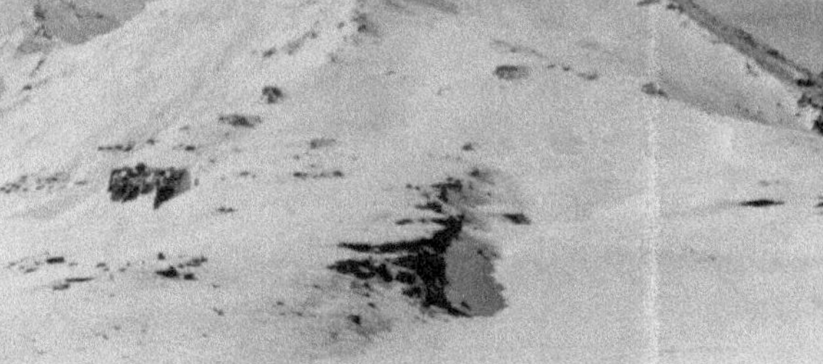

Views of the mountain to the East of the Rohtang Pass

First view of the mountains of Lahoul

The Gephorn (to the north of Sissu)

The Kulti Nala from the south

South of Khoksar

Khoksar Nala

Lahouli Nala

The Chamba Valley below Khoksar

Towards the Rohtang Pass from Khoksar

Shikar Beh and Mukar Beh

An unknown glacier and mountain to the west of Shikar Beh

North of Keylang

Near Gondla

West from the alp above Gondla

The Darche Nala from the main valley

Looking NE from above Keylang

The Bhagat Valley below Kispa

Side nala at Jispa

Mountains seen from the Darche Nala and from the surrounding slopes

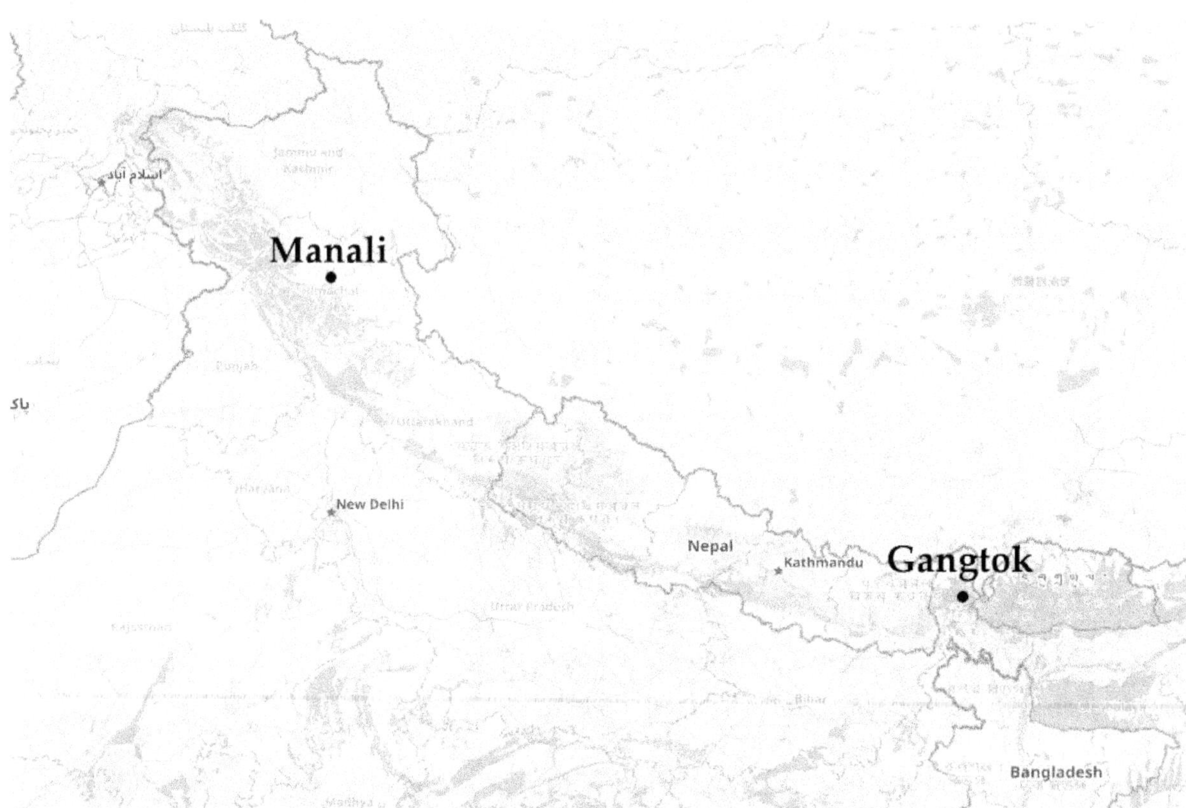

Himalayan area overview

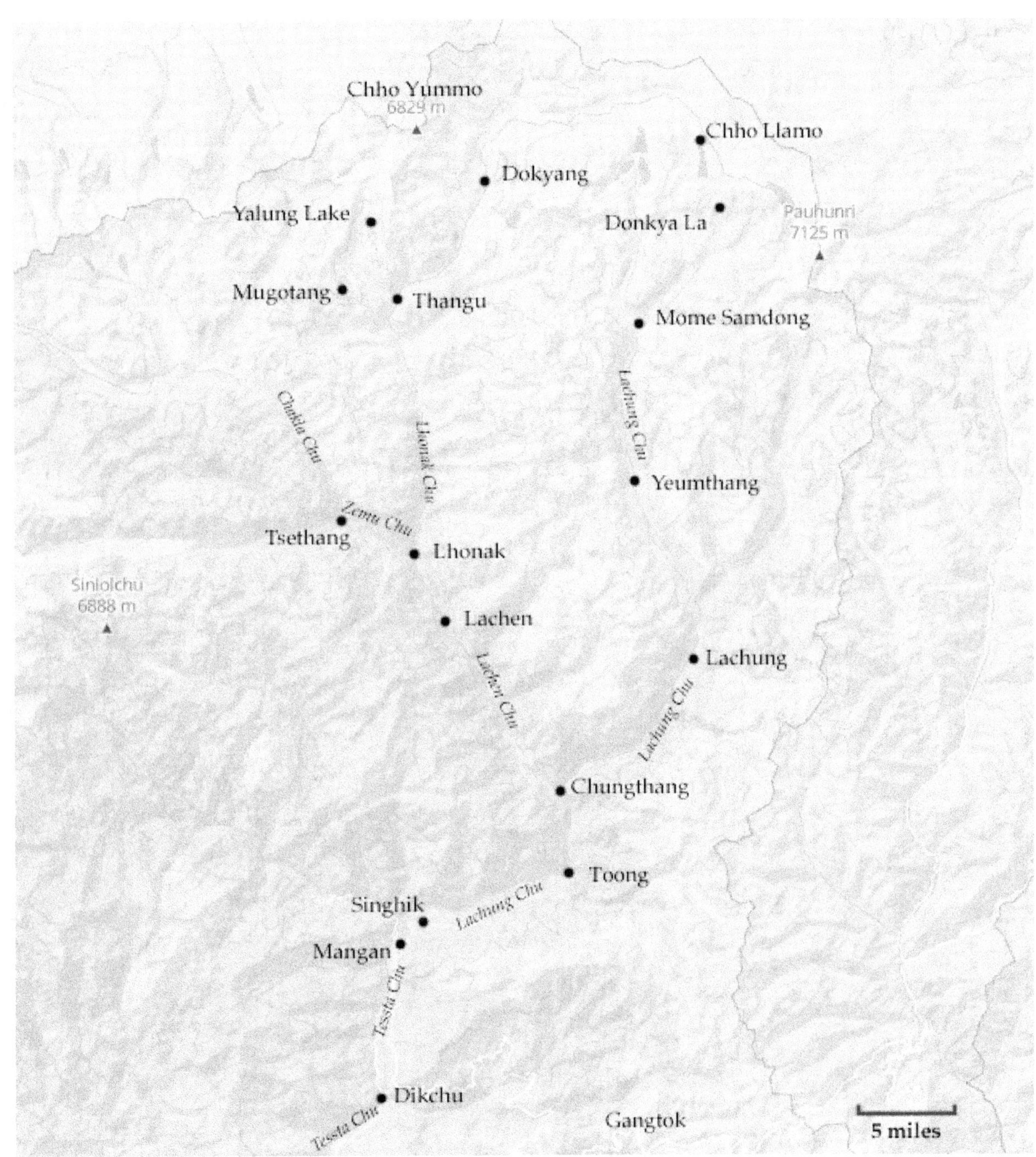

Area covered in Sikkim travels

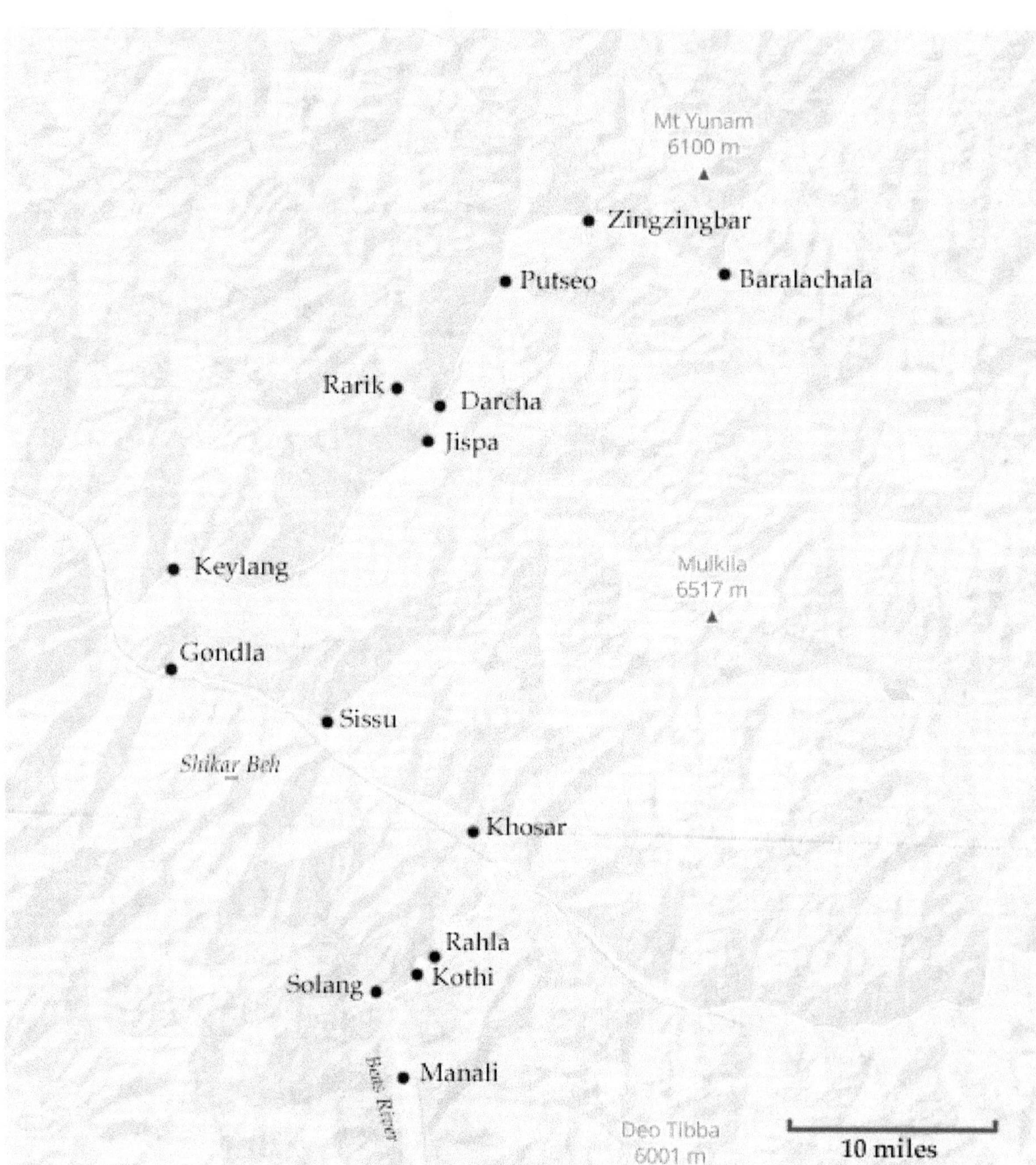

Area covered in Kulu and Lahoul travels

LIST OF ILLUSTRATIONS AND MAPS

AS FAR AS THANGU

Darjeeling 57
The jeep fills up 57
Lorry in difficulties 57
Tista at Tista Bridge 57
Mule 58
Near Gangtok 58
Gangtok 58
A glimpse of things ahead 58
Tista at Dikchu 59
A goat eats up the garden 59
Mangan 59
Paddy fields 59
Tista at Toong with man on the cane bridge 60
CBS crosses a small slide 60
Bridge at Lachung 60
Lamas at Lachung 60
Gorge cut by the flood 61
North from Yeumthang 61
Flood plain above Lachung 61
Dawn at Yeumthang 62
Above the path 62
The road to Mome Samdong 62
Grazing yak 62
On the way to the Sebu La 63
Tibetan yak at Mome Samdong (2) 63
Chombu 63
Donkya Rhee 63
Glimpses of Pauhunri (2) 64
'Allsopps' rests beneath the Donkya La 64
Camp at 17,000' (2) 65
On the way from Dokyang to Thangu (2) 65

THANGU TO THE END

From Thangu 66
Kanchenjunga & Tent Peak 66
Foot Tent Peak 66
3 views of Siniolchu from the Chakla Chu 67
Kanchenjunga & Tent Peak 67
To the East of the The La 68
Chho Yummo 68
A Tibetan Dzong beside the Chakla Chu 68
From the Chakla Chu 69
Chho Yummo 69
From Thandu La 69
From a little lower down 69
Peak to the South of the Metong La 70
Nearly-Tibet (Natu La) 70
Lachsi from Birthday Camp 70
From a spot just inside Tibet to the NW 71
Due W 71
To the S 71
And where we came in, Thandu La 71
Looking forth to Tibet from below the Thandu La 72
Birthday Camp 72
A peak to the East of the Chakla Chu 72
To the South of Thandu La 73
A 1,900' mountain With Thandu La (2,300') on the right 73
View of a portion of Roka from Sikkim 73
View of a portion of Roka from Tibet 73
3 Scenes in the cirque below Rokcha where we should have gone (3) 74
In Lhonak looking up the Khora Chu 75
The Langpo Peaks at Sunset 75
Jonsong and Langpo Peaks 75
Dawn on the snow 75
The dammed-up lake in the Lachen Chu 76
Tomya Cave 76
A chalet in the Zemu Gorge 76
Last sight of a high hill 76
Us (4) 77
And those who did the work 77

KULU AND BELOW

House in the bazaar at Pathankote 127

Mandi: the bazaar 127
Bridge over the River Beas 127
A temple in the garden of the main square 127
A hamlet on the road to Kothi 128
River Beas just above Manali 128
Barley fields above Manali 128
Deserted dak bungalow at Rahla 128
The River Beas 129
Manali, sheep in the Bazaar 129
Flocks of sheep and goats on trek (2) 129
TRANSPORT
By Air 130
By pony (2) 130
By bus (2) 131
By train 131
And by coolie 132
The coolies messing about before setting off for the Rohtang 132
and actually setting off 132
and taking the first of many rests 132
Coolies at work on the way up to the Rohtang Pass (3) 133
And as they more usually appeared 133
LAHOUL
Cow on its way over the Rohtang Pass 134
Cuttting the path over the Rohtang (May 16th) 134
The new bridge over the Darche Nala 134
Blossom in Keylang 134
A stream of mud helps to erode the Darche Nala 135
Opposite Keylang a stream enters a gully white and emerges brown carrying with it a mass of mud and stones 135
Yaks busy ploughing at Gondla 135
A view of North Khoksar from the Rohtang path 136
A Lahoul skyscraper at Gondla 136
A group of houses above Gondla 136
Thakur sahib's house at Kolang 136
Religious procession at the junction of the Chamba and the Bhagat 137
The chorten to which they were going 137
On the road up to Keylang 137
PEOPLE
He who thought it was worth Rs1,100 138
The sirdar 138
The chowkidar of the bungalow at Kispa 138
Fish out of water—babus from the Ministry of Finance on the march (2) 139
Breasting the summit of the Rohtang (2) 139
Characters met on the wayside between Sissu and Gondla 140
Children at the bungalow at Jispa 140
And the most inquisitive of the bunch 140
MOUNTAINS
Looking towards the Rohtang Pass from the South 141
Views of the mountain to the East of the Rohtang Pass (2) 141
First view of the mountains of Lahoul 141
The Gephorn (to the north of Sissu) 142
The Kulti Nala from the south 142
South of Khoksar 142
Khoksar Nala 142
Lahouli Nala 143
The Chamba Valley below Khoksar 143
Towards the Rohtang Pass from Khoksar 143
Shikar Beh and Mukar Beh 144
An unknown glacier and mountain to the west of Shikar Beh (2) 144
North of Keylang 145
Near Gondla 145
West from the alp above Gondla 145
The Darche Nala from the main valley 146
Looking NE from above Keylang 146
The Bhagat Valley below Kispa 146
Side nala at Jispa 146
Mountains seen from the Darche Nala and from the surrounding slopes (3) 147
MAPS
Map of Himalayan area overview 148
Map of area covered in Sikkim travels 149
Map of area covered in Kulu and Lahoul travels 150

www.ingramcontent.com/pod-product-compliance
Lightning Source LLC
Chambersburg PA
CBHW081141300726
48982CB00006B/1034

9780957662827